Country Life Guides

DRAGONFLIES
AND
DAMSELFLIES
of Britain and Northern Europe

Bob Gibbons

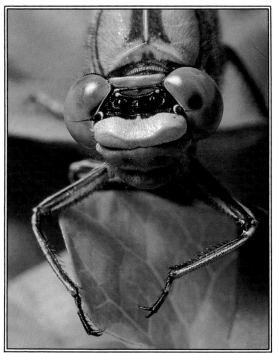

NEWNES ▣ COUNTRY LIFE BOOKS

TO LIZ, WITH THANKS

Acknowledgements

It is a pleasure to acknowledge the help of various people in the production of this book. Graham Vick went to considerable trouble to check the manuscript, and correct a number of errors, for which I am very grateful. Any remaining errors are entirely my own. Rees Cox, Tom Leach and Francis Rose kindly told me of European sites and lent maps and information and Tom Leach also loaned many of his superb photographs. Peter Wilson made an excellent companion on field trips through France and Germany, as well as providing many photographs and snippets of information. Ian Johnson, and Mike Read and colleagues of Swift Picture Library kindly loaned photographs. The difficult and hurried job of typing, partly done over Christmas, was accomplished by Dorothy Jordan and Mary Goodwin. I am also grateful to Jo Barratt for help in collating information, and to Trevor Dolby and Andrew Branson at Hamlyn for much editorial guidance. Finally, I am grateful to my wife Liz for help and support, especially while I was away, during the production of this book, and for drawing all the line illustrations.

R.B.G.

Published by Country Life Books an imprint of
The Hamlyn Publishing Group Limited,
Bridge House, 69 London Road, Twickenham, Middlesex,
England and distributed for them by
Hamlyn Distribution Services Limited,
Sanders Lodge Estate, Rushden, Northants, England

First published 1986

ISBN 0 600 358 410 (softcover)
     0 600 333 787 (hardcover)

Printed in Italy

CONTENTS

Introduction

Dragonflies are among the most beautiful and attractive of all insects. They have been called 'the bird watcher's insect', which aptly describes their fascination. Yet, until very recently they were largely ignored by amateur naturalists, and generally believed to be too difficult to identify without the necessity of catching and killing them.

Thankfully, interest has turned away from the limited and specialised interest in dragonflies as cabinet specimens and producers of unusual coloured 'aberrants' to a deeper study of their life-cycles and behaviour, and their role as predators in and around the aquatic environment. This interest has been fostered more than anything by the classic 'New Naturalist' book *Dragonflies*, first published in 1960. It would also be true to say that nowadays most naturalists take a wider interest in all the component species of ecosystems, and there is a strong desire to identify, at the very least, insects without having to catch and kill them. Field guides help fulfil this need to identify, although with dragonflies and most other insects, examination in the hand may be necessary for the identification of some species and occasionally microscopical examination is required. As one becomes more experienced most dragonflies can be identified in the field, even on the wing, by their behaviour, size and general colour. It may be daunting, and even somewhat unbelievable at first, to hear someone pronounce on the identity of a species seen fleetingly 20 metres away, but the more experienced you become, the more you can match the 'jizz' – the whole persona – of the insect with the time of year, habitat, area, rarity value and so on, and come up with an answer that is 99% certain!

Geographical area covered

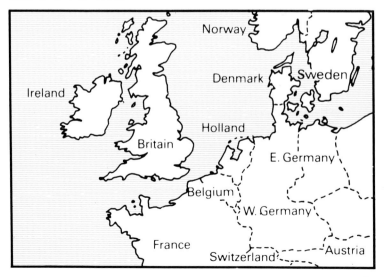

This book is intended as pocketable guide to all the dragonflies regularly seen in the area covered (see map page 5), with colour photographs of most of those species that can be identified in the field or in the hand. Throughout the book the term 'dragonflies' refers to dragonflies *and* damselflies, unless particular distinction is made. The area covered includes Great Britain, Eire, the northern half of France, West Germany, Holland, Belgium, Luxembourg, Denmark and southern Scandinavia, and the book describes the great majority of species for adjacent countries such as Switzerland, Austria, and the East European communist bloc countries such as East Germany.

Life-cycle

To most people, dragonflies are simply attractive and highly mobile winged insects, yet this conspicuous adult phase is only one part – and often a very short part – of a complex life-cycle, of which the greatest part is spent in an aquatic environment, in a lake, pond or stream. An understanding of the life history of dragonflies is crucial not only for anyone studying this group of insects, but also for anyone involved in their conservation, since the adult phase can only be considered and managed for in the context of the pre-adult aquatic phases.

The dragonfly life-cycle may be summarised into the stages: egg; prolarva (pronymph); a series of gradually-growing larval or nymphal stages (instars); and the winged adult. (The terms larva and prolarva will be used in this book, as a result of general usage, though the preliminary stages of incompletely metamorphosing insects are often referred to as nymphs.) It may be noticed that there is no pupal stage as in some other insects such as butterflies, and the larval stages gradually develop characters of the adult until the change from final larval stage to winged adult. This type of development, without the pupal or chrysalis stage, is known as incomplete metamorphosis, although anyone who has witnessed the transition from the drab aquatic larva to the beautiful, coloured adult within a few hours, would hardly agree that the term was apt in this case.

Fig. 1   A typical endophytic egg   A typical exophytic egg

We can begin the life-cycle with the egg. The methods of mating and egg-laying by the female are dealt with later (see page 14), and these vary considerably. The eggs themselves are much less variable, but fall broadly into two types – those that are laid into plant tissue are elongated, while those that are scattered freely or laid into mud are rounded or oval (see fig. 1). The former are laid individually, although many may be laid in the same plant, but the latter may be held together in gelatinous strings (e.g. in *Epitheca bimaculata*) or in individual gelatinous capsules which expand on entering the water and may help to adhere the eggs to suitable surfaces, and prevent them from being washed away.

The time from egg-laying until hatching varies. Some eggs hatch within three weeks, others may take up to two to three months, depending on the species and the conditions and a few will overwinter with little or no internal development taking place.

However the eggs are laid, and however long they have remained as eggs, the next stage is similar for all British and N. European species. What emerges from the egg is a tiny 'legless' worm-like object, quite unlike the later stages of larval growth, known as the pronymph or – more generally nowadays – as the prolarva. Its sole function seems to be to allow escape from the egg case, and the plant tissue or sediment that it lies in, without hindrance by any projecting appendages, and its duration is only a few minutes, or even seconds in the case of eggs laid in loose sediment. In *Lestes viridis*, the females lay their eggs in plants overhanging water, so the prolarval stage may last until the prolarva reaches water, and moulting to the second larval instar may be delayed if the prolarva falls onto a leaf or the bank rather than into water.

Within a few minutes the prolarva moults to the second larval instar, which looks more like the familiar larval shape, and which, though small, can usually be identified to family or even generic level. The second instar may not feed, and may itself only last a few days, before moulting to the third instar, the first of a series of similar but ever-growing stages that the insect will pass through before finally reaching maturity and emerging from the water to become an adult.

The total length of time spent in larval stages and the number of instars that are passed through, varies according to species and according to the conditions. Usually the larva undergoes between eight and sixteen moults before it is ready to become an adult. The length of time that this takes varies from a few months to five years, and there are still not adequate records for most species in the wild to show exactly what happens in each species under a range of conditions. The most rapidly-developing species are usually those of still waters, probably because of the higher water temperatures reached, and perhaps, the better food supplies, and the quickest of all are several damselfly species. *Sympecma fusca* which occurs throughout mainland Europe but not in mainland Britain overwinters as an adult, and hibernated females lay eggs after mating in early summer. By July, the new generation of adults appears after only six to ten weeks in the larva stages. Similarly, the emerald damselfly

The larva of *Sympetrum danae* emerging from a pond to transform into an adult. The skin is already beginning to split

Lestes sponsa spends only about three months in the larval stages, though in this case development is from an overwintered egg. Several dragonflies also complete their larval stages within one year, e.g. the darters *Sympetrum danae* and *S. sanguineum*, and the migrant hawker *Aeshna mixta*, while species such as the hairy hawker *Brachytron pratense*, which usually takes two or more years, has been recorded as completing its larval cycle in under a year in favourable conditions. In the south of Europe a few species have two generations per year in good conditions, e.g. *Crocothemis erythraea*, and the *Ischnura* species.

At the other extreme, some of the larger dragonflies, especially more northern species and those of running water, may take a minimum of two years, with up to five years being recorded. The golden-ringed dragonflies *Cordulegaster boltonii* and *C. bidentatus* which are species of clear running water, including cold mountain torrents, may even take more than five years and there is some evidence that this is also so for some boreal *Aeshna* species, but it is very difficult to gather accurate data in the field on their development. It is interesting to note that in these more slowly-developing species, the adult phase, which is likely to last only one to two months, therefore only represents about one-thirtieth to one-sixtieth of the total life-span, yet it is what we normally consider as 'the dragonfly'.

Eventually, however long it takes, the larva reaches its final instar before emergence of the winged adult. Apart from being larger than preceding stages, the final instar also begins to look different as the larval wing sheaths expand and, in the latter stages, the area of the eyes begins to extend and may ultimately meet in the centre of the head in most dragonflies. An expert familiar with a species or genus can predict when the adult is likely to emerge by the larva's external appearance.

For a few days before the larva emerges from the water to transform itself into a winged adult, its behaviour begins to change. This takes place some time during late spring or summer, depending on the individual species and the weather. The free-living mud dwellers begin to move towards the shallows (if they exist) as a response to the warmer temperatures in the shallows, which speeds up the completion of metamorphosis, although in most ponds it also brings larvae nearer to the shore, ready for emergence. A satisfactory gradient from deeper water through marginal shallows to well-vegetated shore is one of the factors that go to make up a 'good' dragonfly pond. The weed-dwelling larval species, e.g. Emperor dragonfly *Anax imperator*, also tend to move closer to the surface by finding the leaves of floating plants. Clearly, this is a vulnerable phase for dragonfly larvae, and some studies suggest that only 50 per cent that start to metamorphose actually complete the process and turn into an adult.

At some stage, the larvae will begin to leave the water and crawl a short distance to find a secure foothold for emergence. Some species such as the *Sympetrum spp.* emerge mainly in the early morning, and a few dragonflies, e.g. *Leucorrhinia spp.* and many damselflies emerge throughout the day. Emergence at night gives better protection from most predators, especially birds, but it may be hindered or even prevented by low temperatures, and, as a general rule, night-time emergence becomes more prevalent the warmer the climate is, and is almost universal in the tropics.

The larvae of different species tend to emerge in different ways, finding different supports, and this is probably one factor that affects which species occur in a given site. Some species, such as the *Libellula* select tall thin stems

Stages in the emergence of a *Libellula quadrimaculata* adult from its
larval skin (exuvia)

of rushes or reeds; some, such as *Anax* select more solid supports and may at times climb well above the water to find them; others find any vertical or near-vertical support low down amongst marginal vegetation, while a few such as the Gomphid dragonflies (mostly river-dwellers) and some damselflies tend to emerge in a horizontal position. Whatever the timing and technique adopted, the dragonfly has to find a secure place where the adult can emerge from the larval case with enough space to expand its wings without impedance. A proportion will always fail to emerge successfully, perhaps because they fall off at a crucial moment, or there is insufficient room to expand the wings, or because another larva has used them as a support. The process of emergence of the adult from the larva is a very critical and vulnerable phase, and it will fail if anything minor goes awry.

Once the larva has found a satisfactory support, which is usually within a metre or so of the water surface but may occasionally be several metres away, the process of transformation begins, usually with a quiet phase of about an hour (depending on temperature) which may follow a few preliminary wriggles to test the grip of the claws. During this period, the method of breathing changes from one primarily adapted to water (see pages 29–30) to one adapted to air. The subsequent process of transformation is one of the most remarkable events in nature and one that every naturalist should try to see if they can (see page 9).

At first a split appears in the larval case, just behind the head; then the head, thorax, legs and part of the abdomen are withdrawn from the larval case, and, in most species, allowed to hang head downwards supported only by the remainder of the abdomen sitting in the lower half of the larval case. Now that the legs have been withdrawn the emerging adult is only held to the support by the empty skin of the larval legs. This 'resting' position is held for between thirty minutes and one hour, depending on the temperature and species, probably to allow the adult's legs to harden. It is a time of great peril for the dragonfly, as it is quite immobile and defenceless, and more conspicuous than the larva alone. At the end of this period of inactivity, the dragonfly will bend its abdomen upwards to allow it to attempt to grasp the larval case behind its 'head', though often the first few lunges miss. Once grasped, this provides the leverage to extract the remainder of its abdomen, and allow it to hang downwards. At first, both the wings and the abdomen are still shrivelled-looking and unexpanded, but from now on they begin rapidly to fill with blood pumped in under pressure until first the wings and then the abdomen reach their full size, usually in about an hour from the last stage of emergence from the case. Initially, the four wings are held back along the abdomen and they are cloudy and shiny as a result of residual fluid between the layers, not yet dried out. Shortly after this, the dragonfly opens its wings to the normal resting position and the muscles of the thorax begin to vibrate, warming the body up in preparation for flight. Then suddenly, weather permitting, the dragonfly takes off on its maiden flight taking it some tens or hundreds of metres from its place of emergence.

This generalised emergence description best fits the larger dragonflies – the hawkers *Aeshna spp.* or the Emperors *Anax spp.* but it is applicable to all species in everything but detail. Damselflies, and a few dragonfly species, rest with their bodies upright, parallel to the larval skin, while some species emerge onto a flat surface, e.g. the river-dwelling Gomphids often do.

After the adult dragonfly has flown, the empty larval case is left behind, and

The cast skins of dragonflies are called exuviae and can usually be identified to species

this is generally known as the exuvia (plural exuviae). It is a perfect, albeit split, replica of the final stage larva and it is therefore identifiable to species. As we shall see (page 40), the study of exuviae plays an important role in population studies and census work, and it is well worthwhile making a collection of exuviae for reference.

The adult dragonfly

The dragonfly that emerges from the larval case differs considerably from the fully-coloured mature adult, and this early immature state is known as the teneral phase. Most teneral males' colouring resembles the female of the species at this stage, before they attain their resplendent mature colours. This process of coloration takes, on average, about a week depending on the species, the weather, and the amount of flights and meals that the individual takes. It should be noted that coloration of dragonflies is a complex matter, and their visible colours derive from several factors some of which decline in effect, and some of which increase in effect, with age so that the colour changes throughout life. Similarly, for the first day or so, the wings of the teneral dragonfly are much more reflective than those of fully mature insects, due to fluid remaining between the two wing membranes; and the flight is more fluttery and weak.

The pale teneral phase corresponds with a period of sexual immaturity and a distinct behaviour pattern associated only with this pre-mature phase. Following a short maiden flight the newly emerged dragonfly will probably rest again for about twelve hours as the tissues and wings harden further. After this, if conditions are suitable, it will begin to feed on the wing, catching invertebrate prey in its 'basket' (see page 25, fig. 3). At this time it shows a strong aversion to water, so that these first immature days or weeks are spent well away from water. If a water body is encountered, it will be actively avoided. During this period, males and females feed and roost together with no territorial or sexual behaviour evident.

After a week or so, the adults, now fully-coloured, begin to return to water. The males of a species tend to return first, because they become sexually mature more quickly, and individuals may make tentative short visits to water before they are fully mature. When they come back to the water, they can be said to be sexually mature, and their reproductive phase has begun.

From this time onwards, the behaviour of different species or groups varies considerably. Most of the largest dragonflies, especially *Anax* and *Aeshna* species exhibit strong territorial behaviour; that is to say, the male will occupy and defend a stretch of water or bank against intruding males of his own species. In large sites such as lakes or rivers, this territory may be mobile, with a different area being defended each day or part of the day. On small sites, one male of a large species may occupy the whole territory exclusively for the duration of his reproductive life, limiting the number of that species to one pair for that site. On one small pond studied in detail by Moore, observation over a long period indicated that the carrying capacity for species studied was always about 1 *Anax spp.*, 2 *Libellula quadrimaculata* (both dragonflies); 6–11 *Pyrrhosoma nymphula* and 20–36 *Ceriagrion tenellum* (both damselflies), measured in terms of mature adult males. It seems to be typical that the larger the species, the larger the territory the male will defend, but that interspecific territorial behaviour is much more limited. The females of the 'territorial' species are not themselves territorial, and they will normally spend much of the day away from water. When they do appear at water, they are instantly seized by the male of the species, and mating will take place. A few dragonflies, most notably the Gomphids (*Gomphus* and *Ophiogomphus*) seem to have very little territorial behaviour, possibly because they usually occur at low densities, often without marked synchronisation of emergence, and spend much of their time away from water.

Some damselflies, notably the Agrions (*Calopteryx spp.*), also show a territorial behaviour, but to a much more limited degree than the larger dragonflies. Damselfly males are known to defend an area containing some sunny patches, some good perches and an area suitable for egg-laying by the mated female. Around the territory lies a neutral area where there is little reaction between individuals. Other damselflies, particularly the smallest such as the *Ischnura* species seem to exhibit very little territorial behaviour, or if it does take place it is on a very small scale.

The pattern of territorial behaviour varies with the weather and the time of day amongst other things, and is by no means fixed. Most dragonflies roost away from water, though not necessarily far away, and males begin to return to water at some time in the early morning, usually an hour or two after sunrise, depending on the temperature. There they take up perches to defend territory and much of the morning on a fine day is spent in territorial activity against other males, or sexual activity if any females show themselves. In most species, this aggressive behaviour declines in the afternoon and more time is spent feeding than fighting or mating. In most of the larger species, the majority of their time is spent on the wing, rather than making sorties from perches like the *Libellula*, *Sympetrum* and *Orthetrum* species tend to do.

Opposite. A vast swarm of *Libellula quadrimaculata* roosting in a reed-bed by a lake in Eastern Europe

If the weather is bad, the behaviour pattern is quite different; in very poor weather most dragonflies will hardly fly at all, and territorial behaviour is abandoned altogether. In populous sites, many males may roost and loaf together at these times, without any aggression. In sunny but cold weather, dragonflies may be more active but tend to avoid water, and congregate, again without conflict, in sheltered feeding areas in the lee of a windbreak, or along nearby rides or lanes. It is clear that both sun and warmth are important for most species to carry out their full reproductive functions, and this is naturally one of the factors that limits the northward extent of dragonflies.

Mating and egg-laying

All the species in Northern Europe with the sole exception of the damselfly *Sympecma fusca*, have an annual cycle in which no adults overwinter, and the cold period is passed as an egg or larva. Successful reproduction every year is crucial, therefore, to each species to ensure its survival (although a few species seem to have staggered larval emergence over two years, which would allow survival through a year when reproduction fails).

Courtship in dragonflies of Northern Europe is usually minimal or absent, though it may take place in ways too short-lived or too subtle to have been observed. The courtship of the Agrion damselflies (*Calopteryx spp.*) is well-known and frequently observed. The male, on seeing a passing female, responds by spreading his wings out and bending up his abdomen, making him, in effect, broader and more conspicuous. If the female responds by flying down to join him, he then performs a sort of fluttering dance around her, displaying his blue-banded wings (in *C. splendens*) in a beautiful and mesmeric fashion, always keeping his head towards the female. Then, suddenly he lands on her and copulation takes place. The white-legged damselflies *Platycnemis spp.* use their conspicuous enlarged tibias on the hind-legs (see pages 63–64) as signals, when the male dangles them in front of the female in a form of display (though there are also records of this as a threat posture between two males of *P. acutipennis*).

In most species, as we have said, there is little in the way of visible courtship. A male dragonfly, on seeing a female, will immediately fly up to her and grasp the back of her head with his anal claspers (see fig. 2) in flight, unless the female is unwilling (e.g. if she has recently mated) when she will evade his advances and behave unhelpfully. Damselflies act in a similar way, except that the male grasps the female slightly further back, on the neck or prothorax, with his claspers. Most species begin the process while both individuals are in flight, but a few, such as the Agrion damselflies, begin on a perch. Once the preliminary grasping position has been taken up, the act of mating can take place in the air, on the ground or perched amongst vegetation, and it can last a matter of seconds or up to several hours. The processes, and the genital structures involved, are quite unique in the insect world.

Some time before mating takes places, often many hours before, since it may be one of the first acts that the male performs on reaching his perch in the morning, the male dragonfly transfers sperm from his normal genital opening near the end of the abdomen (below the ninth segment) to the unique accessory genitalia situated below the second and third abdominal segments.

Opposite. *Enallagma cyathigera* mating in the 'wheel' position

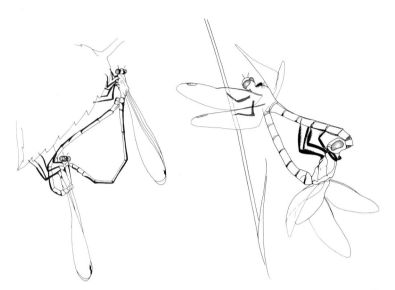

Fig. 2   Damselflies mating in the   Dragonflies mating in the 'wheel'
'wheel' position   position

This is achieved by bending the tip of the abdomen around until it touches the accessory organs, either in flight or when perched. The accessory organs are then 'charged' ready for direct contact with the female copulatory organs, which lie at the tip of her abdomen (below segments eight and nine).

These accessory genitalia consist of a sperm bladder for storage of sperm; a structure which corresponds in function to a penis; and some grasping organs which can grip the female's copulatory organs during mating. Recent research has also shown that one of the functions of this accessory apparatus (in some species) – hitherto somewhat obscure – is to clean out any sperm from previous matings by the female, in her storage receptacles, to ensure that it is the sperm from the male mating at the time that fertilises the eggs to be laid.

Copulation takes place after the male has grasped the female, by the process of her bending her abdomen around so that the genitalia at the tip meet with his accessory genitalia below segments two and three. Sperm transfer by the male may take place rapidly after the male has grasped the female or, as mentioned, at some time previously. The pair are now attached to each other in two points, and this mating position is known variously as 'the tandem position', 'the wheel' and 'the heart position' because of the various shapes or attitudes that may be assumed (see fig. 2 and photograph page 15). In most *Libellula* species mating takes place in the air in a matter of, literally, a few seconds, but in most other species it is more leisurely and may last for an hour or more. Copulating pairs can fly quite readily together, sometimes maintaining the fully mated position, sometimes just attached by the male claspers (anal appendages). The Agrions usually open the circle before taking flight reforming it again on landing.

Egg-laying follows shortly after mating, and it takes place in a variety of ways according to the species involved. Firstly, the behaviour of the male in relation to the female varies. In the *Libellula* species, *Aeshnas* and others, and in the Agrion damselflies, the two partners separate and the female lays alone. In this she may be closely attended and guarded by the male, or she may be left to get on with it. In some species, such as the *Orthetrums*, there is a post-copulatory display in which the male carries out a series of dances to direct and cajole the female to a suitable egg-laying site in his territory. In *Anax parthenope* and *Aeshna affinis* the partners stay together, at least until the beginning of egg-laying though they may separate before this is completed. In other dragonflies, such as the *Sympetrum* darters, and most other damselflies, the pair may remain attached during most or all of the egg-laying procedure.

The egg-laying behaviour itself can be divided into two broad types, although there is variation in style within each of these. One group of species lays the eggs into plants, and this is known as endophytic ovipositing; the other group scatter them freely onto or into the water, and this is known as exophytic ovipositing. These differences are mirrored by a lack of any marked ovipositor in the females of the latter group, and a difference in the shape of the eggs – spherical if scattered, elongated and often pointed if inserted into plant tissues.

The habits of the endophytic species vary. Most of the hawker *Aeshna* species are endophytic, and it is a common sight at a good locality to see a large female *Aeshna juncea* or *A. grandis* on the edge of a lily leaf, or similar, with her abdomen bent tightly round to insert the eggs into the plant stem, using her ovipositor to make an incision for each. The southern hawker *Aeshna cyanea* tends to lay in material just above water level, especially rotting wood, wet moss, or even onto stone or concrete just above water level. The prolarvae from such eggs will need to manoeuvre themselves into the water (unless the water level rises), but observations on such events are rare, and mortality at the prolarva stage may be high for this species.

Most of the endophytic dragonflies oviposit into floating vegetation including moss, and they do not submerge themselves to achieve this. Some damsel-flies behave in the same way, with the female – her male still attached – laying whilst perched on some floating vegetation. Many damselflies, though, will habitually descend the stems of waterplants to well below the water surface before ovipositing, and often the male will descend with her. It is a strange and rather surprising sight when two damselflies disappear slowly below the water, becoming silver as they do so because of the air trapped amongst their body hairs. Pairs of damselflies are regularly recorded as being submerged for 15–20 minutes, and sometimes longer. Representatives of all our damselfly genera except the *Platycnemis spp.* have been recorded laying underwater. In some species the male always separates before submersion, while in *Coenagrion lindenii* the males will submerge but let go if the female goes too deep, and remain hovering above her point of submersion.

The exact significance of underwater immersion is unclear. It may relate to the need to insure against a lowering of water level during the summer, but clearly the same end could be achieved by laying onto floating vegetation, and it is likely that mortality from predation – at a time when it would be particularly damaging to the population – is increased by the habit. The presence of the male, either attached or close-by must aid in bringing the female to the

Red-eyed Damselflies, *Erythromma najas*, descending below water as a pair to lay eggs into submerged plant tissue

surface and preventing mortality through waterlogging. The actual pattern in which the eggs are laid varies according to the species and the plant with some females laying eggs in concentric circles, others in spirals and others more or less at random. Most species do not seem to be tied to the need for a particular plant, though some *Aeshna* species have specific requirements; *Aeshna viridis* a northern boreal species, particularly favours the water-soldier *Stratiotes aloides* for oviposition, and seems to be dependent on its presence in some areas. *Aeshna subarctica*, another northern species, seems to be heavily dependent on the presence of living bog moss *Sphagnum spp.* for ovipositing, even in captivity where most of the more casual dragonfly-plant associations break down.

One species in the area has a quite different endophytic egg-laying strategy. The females of an emerald damselfly *Lestes viridis* (a non-British species, common throughout central Europe) lay their eggs into medium or small sized branches of shrubs near to water. The species of shrub is not usually significant, although willows *Salix spp.* are frequently chosen perhaps simply because they are the most common shrub close to ponds. Usually, mated pairs will take part in the laying process though single females may do so as well, and activity is most frequent in the afternoon. The female makes an incision in the bark and outer layers of the stem and lays the eggs into the tissue, which frequently gives rise to the formation of small galls at each insertion point. The eggs themselves then remain in the plant tissue over the winter, hatching to a prolarva in spring and emerging to fall on or close to the water, as described on page 7. Despite their similarity in appearance and habits, the *Lestes* species described in this book all have different ovipositing tactics, with, for example, *L. dryas* laying into emergent stems just above water level and *L. sponsa* laying most often just at or below the surface.

The remainder of our Northern European species, which includes the majority of the dragonflies (Anisoptera) such as the *Sympetrum*, *Libellula*, *Cordulia*, *Somatochlora* and other *spp.*, lay in a seemingly more casual fashion away from plants, exophytically. Most frequently, the female flies low over the water flicking her abdomen down towards it rhythmically releasing an egg with each flick, at the point of immersion. Sometimes the female appears simply to scatter the eggs from above the water. In either case, the egg-laying micro-habitat seems to be selected with some care – though there is no doubt that many eggs go astray – and females of different species lay in different situations. For example, amongst the darters *Sympetrum spp.*, *S. fonscolombei* tends to select deeper water away from the banks, *S. sanguineum* prefers shallower water with abundant emergent vegetation, while *S. striolatum* tends to select clear water at the outer edge of the marginal vegetation, though such preferences vary according to the site. *Somatochlora arctica* and *Leucorrhinia dubia* tend to oviposit into wet *Sphagnum* or shallow water amongst *Sphagnum* in the acidic pools that they inhabit; whilst other species that may be in the same site, e.g. *Libellula quadrimaculata* or *Sympetrum danae* will probably utilise deeper water or areas with more emergent vegetation.

Clearly this differing egg-laying site-selection gives rise to some separation of the larvae which, though mobile, are likely not to move far from their egg position. The differing sites probably relate to differing larval food and site preferences, though little work has been carried out on this difficult topic.

It is generally true that the exophytic ovipositors lay into still waters in N. Europe, at least, where there is less chance of the eggs being carried away (though it is true, of course, that most endophytic ovipositors also lay in still water!). Nevertheless there are a few exophytic layers that do use flowing water, though none of them ever reach the population densities of still water species, and they have adapted to these more difficult environments by a combination of behavioural and structural differences. The Gomphids, which are primarily species of large rivers with a varied structure, tend to select calm bays and backwaters, with a suitable basal substrate, and, though the eggs are scattered rather than deposited, the majority probably settle to the bottom. *Oxygastra curtisii* selects well-vegetated egg-laying sites which are themselves frequently the calmer stretches, usually on smaller rivers. The *Cordulegaster spp.*, females not only seek out calm sandy stretches on the rather fast-flowing rivers that they inhabit, but they also actively oviposit the eggs into the sediment, using their long ovipositor (actually a pseudo-ovipositor), which must afford the eggs better protection from both predation and the risk of being washed away.

Many of the exophytic species also have a gelatinous coating to the eggs which swells and become sticky on contact with water, and the eggs therefore become attached quite readily to plants or other substrates. One species, *Epitheca bimaculata*, lays a large brown lump of eggs which are usually expressed whilst at rest then carried, attached to the abdomen, to a suitable egg-laying site. On contact with the water this lump expands and unrolls into a gelatinous cord some 20–50 cm long, containing a thousand or more eggs, which soon becomes entangled amongst water plants.

Most exophytic species probably lay more eggs than the endophytic species, with a higher mortality and loss amongst the eggs, though they probably have a lower mortality of egg-laying adults since the lengthy endophytic ovipositing process is a dangerous and vulnerable time.

Flight period and length of life

In Northern Europe, there are dragonflies of one species or another in flight for about eight months of the year, from late March in the warmest areas through to early November when the last faded specimens disappear. The only

An Emperor Dragonfly, *Anax imperator*, in flight, showing the slightly curved abdomen

exception to this rule are the damselflies *Sympecma spp.* (one species in Northern Europe, *Sympecma fusca*) which overwinter as adults (see page 54) and although they hibernate, they may become active on warmer winter days, especially further south.

Within this broad period of activity, individual species will normally only be active as adults for a shorter period. Flight periods are given for each species under the appropriate description, but the wide variation of emergence time and cessation of flight according to warmth and site characteristics means that the periods given are longer, for the widespread species, than they are at any given locality.

In the more northerly temperate zones, most species have no more than one generation per year; that is, eggs laid by the earliest adult will not pass through the stages to become adults themselves in that year, and indeed they may not become adult until several years later. A few species, however, are

in contrast to the straight abdomen of the *Aeshna spp.*

able to take advantage of favourable conditions which occur most frequently in the south of the area. In these warmer more southerly areas the adults that mate and lay in the spring and early summer lay eggs which pass through all the larval stages to eventually emerge as adults in that same year. This has been observed to happen in *Crocothemis erythraea, Sympetrum fonscolombei* and a few damselflies, but it is much more difficult to record with certainty than for example in butterflies, so it may often go overlooked.

The further north we go in the area, the more distinctly seasonal most species become. It is usually possible to distinguish 'spring' species which tend to have a reasonably well-synchronised peak emergence round about May, with very few individuals emerging later, e.g. the hairy hawker *Brachytron pratense*, the emperor dragonfly *Anax imperator* and the large red damselfly *Pyrrhosoma nymphula*. Most other species emerge later in the year, around about midsummer and tend to have a less distinct peak of emergence,

21

with newly-emerged individuals being found right through August and even into September. The 'flight season' is thus considerably extended but it refers to the time when examples of that species are found on the wing, and does not necessarily correspond to the length of life of individual dragonflies.

This raises the question: how long does an individual dragonfly live? Naturally enough, there is considerable variation in the answer, both between species, and within species, and not enough work has been done to allow the formulation of any universal rules. For the spring species, with their relatively synchronised emergence, the length of life is not very different to the observed flight period, since a high proportion of individuals are of the same age. In one study, on *Pyrrhosoma*, it was shown that the maximum age reached by any individual was about 47 days, but that some 50 per cent of individuals had died within a week of attaining sexual maturity (i.e. at about three weeks after emergence). In other studies, it has been shown that *Anax imperator* and *Aeshna juncea* may live two to three months, and it is highly likely that aged individuals of *Sympetrum striolatum* found in November will have reached at least this age.

There seems to be no particularly clear indication that dragonflies live longer than damselflies, or vice versa, though it is likely that the less-synchronised summer emergers would need to live longer to ensure adequate reproduction than the synchronised spring emergers whose adult activities may be completed within three weeks, weather permitting.

The exception to these estimates of longevity is provided by *Sympecma fusca* which does not occur in Britain but is widespread on mainland Europe. They emerge in July and fly until about November, from when they hibernate intermittently in scrub or woodland until March or April. Mating takes place in April and May, and overwintered adults may be seen until June. Thus, most individuals live for ten months, and a few live for almost a year.

Migration and dispersal

Dragonflies and damselflies vary enormously in their capacity for dispersal and travel, but even the smallest and seemingly weakest species can move surprising distances. Still waters are inherently short-lived, and an ability to find new sites, even if only in occasional years of high population or favourable circumstances, must have always been important. Territorialism, at least in the larger species, favours dispersal and it is well-known that the counts of fresh exuviae at a site can exceed the maximum numbers of adults seen by a ratio of at least 100 to 1 (see page 39) indicating a very considerable dispersal (and, perhaps, adult mortality).

Some species of dragonflies and damselflies survive mainly in newly-created or changed sites, e.g. *Orthetrum cancellatum* and *Ischnura pumilio*. Such species must travel significant distances regularly since they normally become extinct locally as a habitat matures. In the last few years, *Lestes dryas* has appeared at a number of sites in south and east England, at many of which it was apparently not present before. Since it was believed to have been extinct, or almost so, in Britain immediately prior to this, the new populations may have come from continental Europe, with the considerable sea-crossing that this must have involved.

A few dragonflies regularly undertake extensive migrations, occasionally in very large numbers. These are not normally bi-directional outward and return migrations, but are rather the movement of large numbers of individuals away from their site of origin, often never returning. *Hemianax ephipigger* is an Aeshnid dragonfly whose breeding grounds are in north Africa, south Asia and the extreme south of Europe, but individuals are occasionally encountered throughout Europe, and on several occasions it has reached Iceland, the only dragonfly recorded from that country. The four-spotted chaser *Libellula quadrimaculata* is common and widespread throughout Northern Europe, but in some parts of Europe, especially eastern Europe, it may reach enormous numbers in good seasons. Records of mass migrations of *L. quadrimaculata* date back many hundreds of years, and in 1862 a migration of this insect over Germany was estimated to contain about 2400 million individuals, all travelling westwards. Similar migrations have been recorded regularly since, though numbers seem to be declining. Records of such migrations also exist for *Sympetrum striolatum*, *S. meridionale* and others, though rarely on quite such a spectacular scale. It is rare for Odonatologists to be in the right place at the right time to study these periodic mass movements, though Longfield records witnessing a major migration of *S. striolatum* in 1947 on the southern coast of Ireland, estimated as at least a million insects, and lasting several weeks.

Other dragonflies regularly migrate outwards from their main breeding areas, in less spectacular numbers, but it is perhaps more significant because it takes place annually and allows colonisation of new habitats. *Crocothemis erythraea* and several *Sympetrum* species regularly migrate out like this although the scale may vary.

The causes of migration in dragonflies are still poorly understood, and it is probably unwise to look for any single causative factor. The smaller-scale regular migrations probably depend upon a combination of a high level of synchronised emergence, a shortage of food, winds in a suitable direction and other factors leading to a rapid and partially directional outward migration.

The larger mass migrations may have more complex causes. Recent research suggests that dragonfly populations may interact cyclically with a trematode worm, for which the dragonfly is a secondary host. In contrast to the usual population build up and crash, out of phase with the parasite, a more subtle mechanism is proposed in which the dragonflies become increasingly aggravated by the parasite leading to an increased tendency to migrate. This idea is supported by the regular approximately ten year cycles of migration often observed. There is also some evidence that dragonflies present in large numbers may undergo physiological changes, rather like locusts, causing them to migrate. Whatever the final trigger, it is clear that a prerequisite is a very large adult population, often, although not necessarily, with a high degree of synchronised emergence, and a shortage of available resources.

Flight and feeding behaviour

No-one who watches dragonflies can fail to notice that they are accomplished and skilful fliers, with great speed and agility. These aerobatics are especially evident when feeding – they are the falcons of the insect world preying on all other flying insects, catching them on the wing.

A Small Red Damselfly, *Ceriagrion tenellum*, with prey, held in its 'basket'

Dragonflies and damselflies have four wings, in two pairs, like most other insects, which can beat independently of each other when required. Whilst most insects move their wings by changing the shape of the thorax (to which the wings are attached) by internally attached muscles, dragonflies differ in having muscles attached directly to the wings, rather like birds, providing most of the motor force for flying. We have already seen that dragonflies can fly vast distances during mass migrations, and some of the larger hawkers spend most of any sunny day on the wing. They can also fly very fast; such accurate records as have been made suggest that our larger species can fly at up to about 30 km per hour and there are records for non-European species of up to twice this speed. Damselflies are much slower and less direct in their flight with recorded speeds of 2–3 km per hour, but both groups are able to fly backwards with ease or remain in one place for long periods of hovering. The larger dragonflies, such as *Aeshna grandis* can also glide and sail, gaining or losing height according to the updraughts and their attitude. Most dragonflies achieve these capabilities with a relatively slow wingbeat of about 30 beats per second. This can be audible as a pulsating whirr in contrast to the continuous whine of insects with faster wing beats. The larger dragonflies are very audible when they twist and turn, but less so when flying straight.

The dragonfly appears to keep its balance throughout the difficult manoeuvres it performs, including flying in tandem, with the aid of its head and eyes which act as a balancing organ.

In almost all the species in the area, activity is diurnal – they fly during the

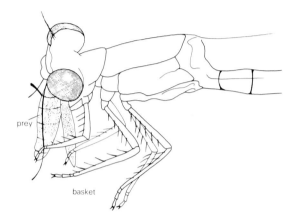

Fig. 3 Damselfly with prey, showing the use of the 'basket'

daylight hours, and they are also heavily dependent on the weather. Low light intensity and low temperature will ground virtually all individuals (which clearly limits their capacity for reproduction in poor summers), while others need one or other to be higher. Some *Aeshnas*, such as *A. cyanea* and *A. juncea* will fly well on into evening, and even into the early darkness, but only if the air is warm. In the tropics, this habit is much more frequent, and even in southern Europe, evening flying is observed more often, because of the higher air temperatures.

Feeding behaviour and mechanisms are generally the same throughout the north European Odonata. Their prey is almost wholly confined to flying insects of various sorts, all caught on the wing, by visual perception. The legs of dragonflies are long and bristly, and, because of the tilted thorax and their differing lengths, all six will meet at a point if they are held forwards. This modification allows the formation of a 'basket' in which prey is caught from the air, and then grasped by the mandibles (see fig. 3), and dismembered as necessary. The prey items are very varied, and will include any insects that occur in the feeding area which the individual can handle. Thus the larger dragonflies will include butterflies, other dragonflies (especially teneral ones) and damselflies, moths, flies, and representatives of most other groups, though difficult or distasteful species, such as wasps, hornets or scarlet tiger moths may be actively avoided.

There are two distinct strategies for catching prey. The larger dragonflies, particularly the Aeshnid family and the golden-ringed dragonflies *Cordulegaster spp.* catch their prey whilst on the wing, and devour it in flight unless it is particularly large or awkward. The Libellulidae and all the damselflies, in contrast, tend to make sorties from perches in pursuit of prey as it is sighted, and they return to their perch, or a nearby one, to devour it. At this stage, it may be quite easy to approach a feeding individual. The enormous eyes, which in some dragonflies take up over half of the surface area of the head, are central to the feeding strategy allowing detection of prey from considerable distances over a very wide area of vision. Some species can detect prey up to 20 metres away, and can detect marked movements at over double that distance. It is little wonder that they are difficult to approach and photograph or catch when they are active!

Dragonfly parasites and predators

No totally complete study of the mortality at each stage of the dragonfly life-cycle has ever been attempted, and possibly never will be in view of the problems of studying the aquatic stages. Nevertheless, we do know something of the range of predators and parasites that can attack and kill dragonflies at their various stages, and these are many and varied.

The egg is vulnerable to many aquatic omnivores, such as snails, some of which may eat them inadvertently whilst feeding on plants. The *Hymenoptera*, an order which encompasses parasites of almost all other insects, includes a minute wasp *Anagrus incarnatus* and other fairy flies (Mymarides) which lay their eggs into the eggs of dragonflies. The developing larva of the wasp feeds on the developing egg, and a wasp emerges instead of a dragonfly, swimming to the surface with the aid of its wings.

The larvae are parasitised, though not killed by, a trematode worm *Prosthogonimus* for which birds are the main host, and transfer is only effected if the larva or adult is eaten by a bird. Perhaps the presence of the parasite increases dragonfly mortality by slowing them down, making predation more likely. Another species, *Gorgodera amplicava*, has water snails and amphibia as alternate hosts. Larvae are eaten by a wide range of predators: when they are small, in the early stages, water-beetles (Dytiscids), water scorpions (*Nepa cinerea* and others), back-swimmers (Notonectids), and other aquatic insects, and newts and fish, such as trout and bream both as adults and younger fish, eat them whatever the size of the larvae. Bottom-feeding ducks take some, and small aquatic carnivorous mammals such as the water-shrew feed on them. Studies in the USA by fisheries biologists have indicated that the larvae may form up to 70 per cent of the diet of one species of bass, and 14 per cent of the food taken by a diving duck.

As the larvae prepare for emergence and move to the shallows, they become vulnerable to other predators since they are readily visible from the surface. A friend who is a bird photographer and entomologist was photographing bluethroats at the nest in Hungary and became so engrossed in watching the pair bringing nothing but larvae of *Libellula quadrimaculata* for the young, that he forgot to take any photographs! There are also records of predation by herons, egrets, coots, moorhens and other birds that feed in the shallows. As they emerge from the water, and the final moult to winged adult takes place the larvae/adults remain immobile for several hours, frequently in the daylight and often somewhere quite conspicuous, and inevitably they fall

Opposite. Reed Warbler feeding an *Ischnura elegans* to its young

Damselflies, such as this Large Red Damselfly, are frequently trapped by sundews in boggy places

prey to a wide range of carnivores and omnivores. Much depends on the situation where emergence takes place, and it is well-known that even birds such as house-sparrows can quickly learn that emerging damselflies are food if the pond is close to a sparrow colony. Regular predators at this stage include wagtails, ducks and blackbirds; Corbet, for instance, studying *Anax imperator*, found that a pair of blackbirds ate 133 emerging or teneral adults in one year, and 146 the next, representing a significant impact by just one pair of birds, raising a brood. Interestingly, though, he found that a higher mortality was caused, in both years, by an incomplete expansion of the wings (4·3 per cent and 8·9 per cent in the same two years respectively).

Once the teneral dragonflies take flight, a new range of predators appears. These mainly comprise insectivorous birds, of which the most frequently-recorded are flycatchers, bee-eaters, wagtails, reed and sedge warblers, cuckoos, hobbies, red-footed falcons, swallows and martins, and even black-headed gulls. Where such birds are rearing young near a dragonfly site, the adult dragonflies can form a considerable part of their diet for the summer period. The weaker flight of tenerals, closer to the ground, makes them more likely to become entangled in the larger spider's webs, and such webs are often filled with tenerals at emergence periods in sites where Odonata are abundant. Tenerals, and damselflies of any age, are liable to get caught on the sticky hairs of the insectivorous sundews *Drosera spp.* which are common on damp acid peaty sites where many dragonflies thrive.

The winged stage also has parasites living on it. A well-known and widespread example is the water-mite *Arrenhurus ornatus* which collects on the wing sheaths of the emerging larva, passes to the thorax of the adult where it sucks fluid from the body, and then drops off after the dragonfly's maturation period, when it returns to the water, so using the teneral phase of the dragonfly as a means of dispersal. There are also minute parasitic flies or midges (Ceratopogonidae), such as *Pterobosca paludis*, which attach themselves to the wing-veins and suck blood from them.

Finally, mention should be made of insect predators, of which the main ones are probably dragonflies! It is quite frequent for large species to catch and eat smaller ones, or even for adults to eat teneral individuals of the same species. Damselflies, in particular, are also preyed on by other insects, such as the robber-flies (Asilidae).

The larval stages

The stages in the life-cycle leading up to adulthood have already been described, but little has been said of the biology or ecology of the larval stages.

The larva is wholly aquatic in European species from prolarval stage to emergence to become an adult, and this phase lasts from between two months or so to several years. The structure of the larva varies between species and distinctive groupings can be readily recognised, though the major difference lies between the larvae of damselflies and those of dragonflies. All are highly predatory, but in structural and physiological ways, they differ somewhat.

The larvae of the damselflies (Zygoptera) are slender relatively graceful creatures (see fig. 17), with three long blade- or leaf-like caudal appendages ('tails'). These appendages are external gills, and gaseous exchange takes

A typical damselfly larva, clearly showing the three caudal lamellae (gills)

An Aeshnid larva showing a side-view of its mask hinged in below its head

place externally, at their surface. If lost early on, they may regrow, but later instars appear to be able to survive without them, and clearly some gaseous exchange takes place directly through the skin. These caudal lamellae also aid the larva in swimming, which it achieves by flapping its abdomen and the attached gills from side to side, with the gills giving additional propulsion. They also move around by crawling.

The dragonfly (Anisoptera) larvae have a different structure (see fig. 18). They are larger and usually much squatter, with some genera being very broad. There are no external gills, and instead there is an elaborately convoluted, almost lung-like structure within the rectum, known as the 'branchial basket'. Water is pumped in and out of the rectum and gaseous exchange takes place at the greatly enlarged surface area of this 'basket', which is a unique structure among the insects. This pumping mechanism is also used to effect movement: water is taken into the rectum and then, when necessary, expelled with force to provide a form of jet propulsion, moving the larva rapidly over a short distance.

So, dragonfly and damselfly larvae are readily distinguishable from each other despite the differences within each group. Both, however, share another remarkable and unique feature, known as the 'mask', used to catch prey. The lower lip (labium) of the larva is greatly enlarged and armed with strong hooks, and when not in use it is folded downwards and backwards beneath the head (see fig. 4). When prey is seen, the whole structure is shot out at lightning speed by hydrostatic pressure, grabbing the victim whilst still up to a centimetre or so away. The unfortunate prey is then brought by muscular action back to the mouth hooked in the arms of the mask, and consumed.

The prey that larvae will catch varies enormously, according to the instar stage, the availability of food, and the species of dragonfly. Generally, most species will eat any form of animal life that they can catch; this varies from very small prey such as protozoa or small crustacea for the earliest instars and

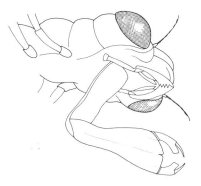

Fig. 4   Dragonfly larva (*Aeshna spp.*) mask, partially extended

The larva of the Golden-ringed Dragonfly *Cordulegaster boltonii* from the front showing its fearsome mask

smaller species, through to sizeable items such as fish fry and tadpoles for fully-grown large larvae such as *Aeshna* or *Anax*. One estimate was made, in 1937, to the effect that a population of *Anax* larvae could halve the number of fish in a breeding pond, though this is of dubious accuracy. The main animals that escape predation seem to be those that move too slowly to be detected.

The larvae of different species by no means occupy the same niche, even when in the same habitat, and to some extent both their structure and their feeding behaviour relate to these differences in microhabitat. The most conspicuous and best-known of Odonata larvae are those that live up amongst the weed growth, in the light and warmth of the top layers of water. Many of the species found in this book fall roughly into this category, and it includes most of the damselflies together with *Anax*, *Aeshna*, *Sympetrum*, and *Leucorrhinia*. Such species are more agile, more lithe, and frequently have larger eyes than those species that dwell on or amongst the bottom mud. These species 'hunt' their prey actively, and there is a record of an *Aeshna juncea* larva watching and moving in concert with some tadpoles in another tank some 10 cm away.

At the other extreme are the species that live wholly or partially amongst the basal sediment of the water body – the mud-dwellers. These include *Gomphus* and its relatives, the *Cordulegaster* species and the *Orthetrums*. They are slow-moving, squat and unattractive, frequently with reduced eyes on projections on top of the head. The abdomen may be curled around to project above the mud surface – allowing unhindered respiration – and only this and the eyes are visible. Such observations as have been made on these larvae indicate that their feeding is much more clumsy and passive than that of the weed-dwellers, relying on prey to come to them. As a general rule, these mud-dwellers develop more slowly than the more active weed-dwellers. A few species, such as *Calopteryx* and *Platycnemis* fall uneasily between these two groups, and their habits are not completely clearly defined.

Many species pass the winter in the larval stage. Most larvae become less active as the temperature drops, and they are much more difficult to locate in winter, though they do not hibernate, becoming active whenever conditions permit. Some remarkable records of the hardiness of larvae exist, and many species are known to tolerate being frozen solid for prolonged periods, though rapid intermittent freeze and thaw may be more damaging. They can also survive periods of drought when their habitat dries out completely.

The larvae of dragonflies and damselflies may lack the charisma of the fully-coloured winged adults, but they are fascinating subjects for study, with the advantage of being present all the year round. With practise, all the species can be identified from late instar larvae, making any study that much more rewarding.

Dragonfly habitats

Because dragonflies have both a long aquatic phase and a predatory aerial phase (the adult), their habitat requirements are complex. They are inevitably tied to their larval habitats, which are always wetland of some form or another, but the adults themselves have additional requirements which must be satisfied, especially with larger species. A satisfactory 'hinterland' of good hunting habitat with perching places, shelter, warmth and lack of pesticides

Unpolluted lowland rivers, with a slow flow and abundant vegetation, will usually support several species

may make an enormous difference to an otherwise basically suitable larval site. Some species are closely confined to one particular set of conditions, while others may be successful over a wide range of habitats. Some may be very pollution-sensitive, whilst others may be relatively pollution-tolerant. There is a general tendency for species to become more demanding away from their centre of distribution and for most dragonflies this 'centre' is towards the south. So, some of the closely-defined conditions needed by species further north break down in the south of the area.

Flowing water

Flowing water, unless very sluggish – such as in old canals or obstructed ditches – is not an optimal dragonfly habitat and rarely supports large numbers of species or individuals. Some dragonflies are specifically adapted to flowing water, and may be confined to it as a larval habitat, but these are relatively few.

Little-used canals, especially where they widen into 'flashes', may be rich dragonfly habitats

They include the *Cordulegaster spp.* which live in faster-flowing, often acidic well-oxygenated waters (though not too fast-flowing); and the Gomphids which, with the exception of *G. pulchellus*, tend to favour large slow-flowing, often quite silty rivers, with shallows, mud-banks and calm areas. In Britain, the only *Gomphus G. vulgatissimus*, is almost confined to the major river systems, such as the Thames and Severn, but in continental Europe, such rivers are more widespread. Although a relatively high silt load is tolerated, there is a distinct requirement for a natural and varied river course, with calm areas, bays, pools, backwaters, sandbanks and unimproved bankside vegetation. Such conditions are most readily found in large rivers such as the Loire; those that are canalised are usually unsuitable. Such rivers are usually also good for *Calopteryx spp.*, with *C. virgo* preferring the more acid and rather smaller faster-flowing rivers, and *Platycnemis pennipes* and *P. acutipennis* may also occur. On continental rivers, especially in France, there may be a wider range of species breeding in rivers including *Orthetrum cancellatum*, and *O. coerulescens*, and damselflies such as *Erythromma najas*, and various *Ischnura* and *Coenagrion* species. Almost any still-water species can occur if there are enough calm, clear areas in the river.

Slow-moving but small, clear rivers or brooks are good dragonfly habitats, and this is the most likely habitat for the beautiful and rare *Oxygastra curtisii*, which may also occur occasionally in canals and lakes. In Britain, it occurred on the Moors River in Dorset, a smallish river of varying acidity, but it became extinct when slight pollution occurred (see page 112), and it is clearly a highly sensitive species. Such habitats are also suitable for some Gomphids, especially *Ophiogomphus* and *Onychogomphus* species, all of which tend to prefer sandy rather than silty rivers. *Calopteryx splendens* and the *Platycnemis* species also occur in this type of habitat.

The highest reaches of watercourses, such as springs and small rivulets may support different species. Further north, *Ischnura pumilio* favours bog or fen areas with moving water – 'flushed' areas. *C. mercuriale* on the other hand seems to prefer calcareous waters, and *I. pumilio* may also select such areas at times. *Orthetrum coerulescens* uses these areas, and *Cordulegaster boltonii* is often seen on very small streams where the flushes or springs begin to collect into a flow.

Old, unpolluted and slow-moving canals, that are not much used by boat traffic, may be very good dragonfly habitats, especially if there are regular flashes or turning areas, and calmer patches. Some species, such as *Coenagrion lindenii*, *Oxygastra*, the *Platycnemis* species, and *Libellula fulva* (if further south) particularly favour such habitats, but good examples with all the right features may support a very wide range of species, including, quite often, the beautiful emerald *Somatochlora metallica*.

Fast-flowing torrents support virtually no dragonflies in this area, except the *Cordulegaster* species, especially *C. bidentatus*, and only then if there are some calmer areas with a sandy or silty base.

Still waters

Still waters are the dragonfly habitat *par excellence* where dragonflies reach their greatest abundance and diversity. The term encompasses an enormous variety of habitats such as lakes, farm ponds, old gravel pits, mountain tarns, ditches, bog pools and others with great variation in size, pH, stability, clarity, temperature, salinity, depth, sunshine, food availability, presence of predators, and surrounding or emergent vegetation, as well as the habitat that the water is set amongst. The factors which determine the quality of the water are more important than the category of the water or its origins, in attracting dragonflies. Size in itself is not especially important except in so far as it affects shelter and wave formation, though large lakes are often not especially rewarding places to look, for these very reasons, unless they have abundant sheltered bays and shallows coupled with adequate emergent vegetation. Smaller lakes tend to fulfil the necessary criteria better, though there are exceptions such as some of the large 'etangs' in the Brennes area of France. Shelter and a good range of emergent, marginal and aquatic vegetation are very important for most species, and the best still water sites usually have all these features since, collectively, they allow food and cover for the larvae, a range of emergence sites, abundant perches for all the differing requirements (from lily pads for *Erythromma*, and reeds for *Orthetrum* and *Libellula* to trees and bushes for *Aeshnas* to perch and mate in, or *Lestes viridis* to lay into). These factors are amongst the most important for any site, though of course they themselves interrelate with other factors such as depth, pollution and pH.

The pH (a measurement of base status, i.e. acidity or alkalinity) may be important to some species in some areas. In Britain, especially in the south, mildly acidic lakes provide the most important dragonfly sites in terms of

The optimum dragonfly habitat is warm, shallow, well-vegetated still water with adequate shelter

numbers of breeding species. If the water is too acid, as it may be in the uplands or on very acid soils, the number of species is limited to those few that are tolerant of this, e.g. *Libellula quadrimaculata*, *Ceriagrion tenellum*, or *Aeshna juncea*, and the further acidification of already acid waters by 'acid rain' may be beginning to reduce the number of species even here. Very strong alkaline lakes such as 'marl lakes' or other high pH waters have a poor dragonfly fauna, though neutral to slightly alkaline lakes may be very good, especially on mainland Europe.

Stability of water regime can be important. Water bodies that dry out annually are unlikely to be good, though a few species will use them, e.g. some Lestids will constantly recolonise them, especially if wet mud (which some larvae will survive in) remains. Marked fluctuations or 'draw-down', such as in reservoirs, is not helpful, mainly through its effect on the marginal vegetation.

Clarity or turbidity, which may often interrelate with pollution, affects dragonfly larvae through food availability, effect on aquatic vegetation and possibly in indirect ways. It is unlikely that very turbid waters will be good for dragonflies, though occasional changes, as after heavy rain, are unimportant. Pollution, and its side-effects, is central to the loss of many dragonflies from our countryside, and is considered in more detail under the section on conservation (see page 41).

Dragonflies have no particular requirement for great depths of water, and most of the best sites are relatively shallow, or at least have large areas that are shallow. Except in the hottest areas, they need warmth, and this is best provided by shallow water with margins that receive full sunlight. Heavily overshaded waters are poor, partly because of the colder shallows and partly because, in small water bodies, the leaf litter causes deoxygenation as it rots, and the water will support little aquatic life. A few species need some trees overhanging, e.g. *Somatochlora metallica* appears to, but not to the point of complete overshading. Some species seem to particularly need shallow water: *Lestes dryas* has a demanding requirement for shallow well-vegetated water in some areas.

Saline water is inimical to most species, but there are increasing numbers of records of species able to breed in brackish waters, including *Orthetrum cancellatum*, *Libellula quadrimaculata* and various damselflies. There is a variation in tolerance of salinity throughout the area, but no species seems to tolerate *very* saline water.

Where predators are at an unusually high level, almost always because of man's activities, then numbers of emerging dragonflies may be drastically reduced, even if other factors are right. Heavily-stocked fishponds are often unsuitable, unless very large and varied, and garden ponds may fail as good sites because of high numbers of sparrows, blackbirds and other garden birds which prey on the emerging larvae.

Finally, the setting of the water body is very important. Waters surrounded by arable fields, industrial land or other hostile situations are unlikely to reach their full potential. In contrast, a good mixture of varied semi-natural habitats, such as heathland, woodland or marsh, with adequate shelter, promotes a stable unpolluted water regime and allows all the needs of dragonflies – the teneral period away from water, feeding, roosting, sheltering, reproduction, dispersal – to be met successfully.

Other habitats

Bogs are a particular type of dragonfly habitat, which may contain still or gently moving water, characterised by the presence of an actively growing bog-moss (*Sphagnum*) surface, a base of peat, and an acid water regime. A large varied bog is frequently of exceptional value for dragonflies, especially where it has open water (including peat-cuttings), a good heathland catchment area, some shelter, and water chemistry that is not too acid. In southern Britain, many of the very best dragonfly sites with up to 60 per cent of the British fauna, are bog habitats. Many of the species use the bog pools in the same way as any other example of acidic standing water, but a few species are particularly associated with bogs, e.g. *Leucorrhinia dubia* prefers the shallows at the interface between boggy pools and a bog surface; and *Aeshna subarctica* lays into the living bog-moss surface, as does *A. caerulea* although to a lesser extent. Incidentally, the food and feeding behaviour of the larvae of these specialised bog species are still largely unknown.

Ditches in marshes or on levels, such as the Somerset levels, or the Pevensey levels in England, and many of the 'Marais' of France can be excellent dragonfly habitats where the agricultural way of life remains as traditional pasture use. Ditches cleared every 5-10 years seem to be best, and the level character of the situation keeps them almost as still water. In Britain, species such as *Anaciaeschna isosceles*, *Brachytron pratense*, *Lestes dryas* and others are especially dependent on ditches, while further south *Libellula fulva*, *Platycnemis acutipennis* and *Gomphus pulchellus* may make use of them.

Overgrown slow-moving ditches support most still-water species as well as a few rarities

Finally, there are various habitats which do not have many of the required characteristics, but which still support some species. Abandoned gravel pits, sand pits and other workings, even before they have developed a reasonable flora, will support breeding populations of *Orthetrum cancellatum* in particular, and *Ischnura pumilio* and *Crocothemis erythraea*, amongst others, in the south of the area. These old workings are becoming important alternative dragonfly habitats as they mature, and large areas of workings may become very valuable. Even less obvious habitats include stone water tanks, washing ponds from tin-mining, and dew ponds, but such sites are the exception rather than the rule, and will not normally support more than a few species.

Studying dragonflies

Apart from the pure pleasure of studying dragonflies, there is much to be gained from their study. Although the broad distribution of all species is well-known, many new sites are still being discovered, even in the most populous and best-known countries. Because of the speed with which sites are being lost, it is essential to find and record these sites before it is too late. Most countries operate a recording scheme for local and national records, and any records, especially but not only of rare species, should be submitted. Many areas of land that are in safe hands and could be managed for dragonflies – including nature reserves – are inadequately studied and recorded for this group, and more work always needs doing. Accurate census work, to determine, for example, the number of dragonflies emerging from a site, is more difficult and has been attempted less often. It is well worth learning to find and identify exuviae (see page 49) which give a much clearer picture of the dragonflies of a habitat, and can be recorded whatever the weather. One investigation, for example, showed that at a pond where no more than a few individuals of *Aeshna cyanea* were seen, at least 1600 adults of this species had emerged. Casual recording might not suggest this site was of much interest, but more detailed recording would.

Monitoring, i.e. the regular recording of numbers of species on a standard-ised basis, over several years, would be very valuable especially if it can be related to management, weather and other external factors. Visits in May, June, July and August, perhaps with one later on should cover all the species, and as far as possible a warm, calm sunny day should be chosen. Counts of adults can be related to counts of exuviae, which may provide a standard ratio for one species.

There is still much to be learnt on the detailed ecology and behaviour of many species, and especially those that occur in more remote habitats, where very little work has been done beyond general recording. Even common species are not fully studied. Work on the aquatic stages is more difficult, but there are more gaps in our knowledge of these stages in the wild, and a fruitful field awaits anyone with easy access to a good breeding site especially if it is an upland or bog site, about which much less is known.

Photographing dragonflies

Nowadays, with a much greater awareness of the need for conservation, and the vastly improved range of equipment available for photographing insects, most people prefer to collect pictures of dragonflies rather than faded dead specimens. Photographing dragonflies is not an easy option, and indeed it presents a considerable challenge to try to portray a range of species adequately – but it can be done, and is highly rewarding.

A single lens reflex (SLR) camera, in which you view through the same lens as you take the picture, is essential for any close-up work. For dragonflies and damselflies, you will need to get close enough to give a reproduction ratio on the film of between ¼ life-size and life-size: that is, the insect will appear on the final negative or slide at somewhere between its actual and ¼ of its actual size. Anything smaller may not give enough information to allow identification and will probably be a less impressive picture. Thus, you need some means of getting closer than a normal standard lens allows, and this can be achieved with close-up lenses, extension tubes, or, best of all, a specialised macro lens. These last are obtainable in various focal lengths from 50–200 mm (for 35 mm SLR cameras), and a macro lens of about 100 mm focal length is probably ideal for dragonfly photography.

Photographs may be taken either by natural light or using electronic flash as the main light source, and each has advantages. If the subject is fairly still (especially in the case of emerging adults) and reasonably large, and the light intensity is high, then natural light is perfectly satisfactory. If you wish to photograph smaller species in close-up, or there is much subject movement, or ambient light levels are low, then a set-up using flash is better. Most photographers prefer to mount one, or better still, two, flashguns on brackets either side of the lens to light the subject evenly and clearly. Exposure metering can be through-the-lens with some camera-flash combinations, or you can calibrate your set-up by trial and error. Because of a convenient factor that ensures that the extra light from the flashes as you move closer is exactly balanced by extra light lost in the lens as you focus it closer, you can be sure of applying your calibrated exposure to most close-up situations. Flashguns held close to the optical axis (including ring-flash) tend to produce distracting reflections in the wings and on metallic bodies, so it is better to hold or mount the flashguns to light the subject more obliquely. A commercially-available system that was designed with dragonflies especially in mind – the Kennett macroflash system – allows flashguns to be held very obliquely at any selected position, and even allows provision for a third flash to light the background evenly. It works extremely well in practice.

With natural light, a medium-speed film of about 100 ASA gives an ideal compromise between good definition and colour and adequate speed. If your subject is very static, such as a large species discovered on a dull day, or an emerging adult in 'resting phase', then the use of a tripod is recommended for maximum sharpness.

Good equipment is of little value if you cannot get close to your subjects. Patience is essential, and your percentage success will be raised by good technique. Dragonflies are the most alert of insects, but a very slow steady approach, in as straight a line as possible, gives the best chance. Minimise any sudden movements and prepare as many camera settings as you can in advance. When looking in likely habitats, keep checking ahead to look for insects on sunny perches or on light patches on the ground, to avoid the frequent problem of seeing them only when they take flight. Late afternoon may be easier for the most mobile species, especially if the weather is sunny but not too hot, when they will tend to bask in suntraps. If you learn your local species' behaviour it helps to find them before they see you, e.g. look for *Aeshna grandis* on vertical trunks or rocks, *A. cyanea* on branches, or *Orthetrum cancellatum* on the ground.

Difficult individuals that settle nowhere near you may be treated in a different way. Set up a telephoto lens, with an extension tube on it if necessary, with your camera mounted on a tripod, pre-trained on any perch that is being regularly used, after observing the best angle to photograph from. If no perches are near enough, you can try providing one.

To get a range of interesting dragonfly pictures, you will frequently need to venture into water. The usual recommendation is therefore for wellington boots, but I find that shorts and plastic beach sandals provide a more versatile outfit for almost any situation. Waders are useful if you are planning to step into deep water, but are a nuisance for general use.

Once you have approached an individual very closely, you may often find that it ignores you unless you move rapidly (beware when winding the film on), and this is then a good time to take a range of close-ups including, for example, the eyes. Make sure that you have enough film in the camera, or with you, before trying to get close to a dragonfly, and that you have any extension tubes or lenses you may require for close-up work. Expect to use a lot of film!

The conservation of dragonflies

The changes that have taken place in the countryside of the countries covered in this book during the last forty years or so have led to dramatic decreases in the variety and abundance of our native flora and fauna. Dragonflies, sadly, are no exception to this, and are amongst the worst hit of all groups, not only suffering a great loss in numbers over most of the area, but with a significant percentage of species becoming extinct in several countries. Dragonflies are beautiful, attractive and interesting creatures, and they are also believed to be sensitive indicators of the general quality of environment, and may be taken as indicators both of the health of an environment and of the likely diversity of other species. They are voracious predators in larval and adult stages, and are therefore dependent on a wide range of other animals; they are, like many predators, very sensitive to pollution; and they are themselves also prey for a wide range of other invertebrates and vertebrates. Their position in the aquatic environment and its interacting surroundings is therefore an important one.

The causes of these declines are manifold and sometimes obscure, but they relate primarily to man's increasing intensity and level of land use, in both obvious and in more subtle ways. Loss of breeding sites is a major feature. Modern technology, and an increased requirement for agricultural and building land, has led to the drainage, infilling, or other forms of destruction of great areas of wetlands on which dragonflies depend. In the UK, for example, it is estimated that, in the last 40 years or so, 50 per cent of lowland fens, valley mires and basin mires have been destroyed or significantly damaged by drainage or pollution, whilst 60 per cent of lowland raised mires have suffered the same fate – and these are all prime dragonfly breeding habitats. In East Anglia, out of the 3,380 square kilometres of fen present in 1637 when drainage began, only ten square kilometres are now left. In France, it is estimated that a staggering 10,000 hectares of wetland are destroyed or damaged each year, mainly for agricultural reasons; and most other countries of western Europe have suffered similar losses. Clearly, such losses in themselves immediately reduce the size of the national dragonfly populations, and some very local and more demanding species become extinct as a result.

More difficult to estimate is the effect of the loss of 'hinterland' habitat where dragonflies feed, roost, shelter, or spend their pre-reproductive phase, and the increasing isolation of sites from each other by hostile situations such as arable land or industry. We know, for example, that in Britain, about 95 per cent of flowery meadows have been converted to sprayed monocultures, and at least 40 per cent of heathlands have been converted to more intensive forms of land use in the last 40 years. The effects of this on the remaining populations is probably significant, reducing their reproductive capacity, their ability to disperse, and the flexibility to survive change.

There is also a more insidious problem; the decline in the ability of the remaining sites to support dragonflies as a result of pollution, eutrophication and management changes leading, in the main, towards homogenisation. Rivers, for example, have not disappeared yet all river dragonflies have declined. The reasons are not simple, nor the same for each species, but they are generally caused by one or more of the following factors: pollution, from industry, housing, sewage or agriculture; increased turbidity from, for example, motorised boat traffic; overstocking with fish coupled with excessive weed management; and alterations in the natural course of the river. River species are adapted to utilising particular 'niches' of the river, frequently calm vegetated shallows, and any flood alleviation, water storage, navigation, or irrigation schemes tend to remove these small-scale features that are so essential.

Still waters have suffered in a similar way. A classic example is provided by the Norfolk Broads in East Anglia which are worth examining in some detail. The 50 or so Broads, legacies of medieval peat-digging, are arguably Britain's largest wetland, spread amongst a vast area of reedbeds, grazing marshes and rivers. Once they were a paradise for dragonflies, and at times the air could be alive with flashes of colour as males clashed, mated and hunted. Some 27 species have been recorded there, including extreme national rarities, and other species that were extremely abundant there. All the Broads and the rivers used to support an abundant and attractive aquatic vegetation, set amidst clear water. But, by the 1960s, many Broads and rivers were becoming turbid and lifeless, and the plants were disappearing. Now, only four out of the 52 Broads support anything like their former richness of plants, and the remainder are almost sterile. *Coenagrion armatum* has gone completely, *Libellula fulva* and *Aeshna isosceles* are almost extinct, while most other species are reduced to a fraction of their former numbers. Yet the Broads themselves, the connecting rivers, and some of the marshland habitat is still there.

The problem is immensely complex, and is still not fully understood: the main causes seem to be increased nitrate and phosphate pollution (from agricultural activities, sewage effluent, and other sources) eutrophication and algal blooms, with greatly reduced water clarity; recreational use by boating craft remains at a high level, and contributes to high silt loads and bank erosion; and a constant conversion of traditional low intensity grazing marshes and reedbeds to arable land which is then regularly sprayed, even from the air, with fertiliser and pesticides much of which end up in the Broads.

Sadly this is typical of the situation in many wetlands which no longer have a natural or traditionally-managed catchment, and the future for such sites is bleak, especially as governmental or public appreciation of the situation usually lags years behind the reality.

There are, however, more optimistic prospects. Interest in dragonflies has never been higher, and this has led to a clearer understanding of their needs. We can now predict the requirements for a wide range of species, and such habitats can be created or maintained to order. Many nature reserves now cater specifically for dragonflies amongst their management plans, and fewer of the foolish mistakes of the past are made. The remnants of extractive industries, especially in high water-table areas, are turning into lakes of considerable value for dragonflies, and in some areas they may support up to 80 per cent of the breeding species in an area (e.g. in Essex, 17 out of 21 breeding species occur in gravel pits). This is clearly good news, though such sites are highly unlikely to cater for the demanding species which require calcareous flushes, unpolluted natural rivers, or shallow lightly-managed ditches, and it is these species that have declined so dramatically.

National and local conservation organisations now take considerably more note of the existence and requirements of dragonflies, and societies and branches of larger societies exist now to further their study. The International Union for the Conservation of Nature and Natural Resources (IUCN) has recognised the threat to dragonfly populations worldwide and has set up an Odonata Specialist Group to advise it on how best to take dragonflies into account.

How to use the species guide

Identifying adult dragonflies: general points

Identifying dragonflies is not particularly easy at first, but it gets easier with practice and experience, and there are some points to bear in mind which will make identification more likely.

Males are much easier to identify than females, if you have a choice. An individual in the hand can usually be sexed immediately by looking for the accessory genitalia under abdominal segments two and three in the males, which are absent in females. In fact, males are more conspicuous and more likely to be caught or photographed than females.

Mature adults are much easier to identify than immature adults or very aged individuals. Tenerals usually have more opaque oily-looking wings than mature adults, and both sexes are frequently coloured similarly to mature females. Some species, e.g. *Sympetrum danae* go through a series of colour changes in their first few weeks of life, and these are described in the text where confusion may occur, though not all can be illustrated.

With practice, dragonflies can often be identified at a distance by the way they fly and perch as well as by their colours. Here a male *Libellula depressa* surveys his territory

Binoculars, preferably lightweight ones of about 8x magnification, are very useful in the field to aid identification once you know what you are looking for. It is useful if the binoculars focus to about 2–3 metres away. If you are less experienced, and cannot get close to individuals that you wish to identify, then it is frequently necessary to catch specimens to examine 'in the hand'. A large black, strong kite net is probably best for this but a folding one is more convenient. Captured insects should be handled very carefully (they damage easily, and larger species may bite!), and examined if necessary with a x10 handlens. It is much easier if you have your identification guide with you at the time.

Before confirming identification, take all the factors into account in addition to just colour, form and size, i.e. check to see if the habitat, distribution, and flight period all fit your species; individuals will turn up in new areas or at odd times, but if all seems wrong, it is likely that the identification is incorrect.

Using the book

Most people will begin by looking at the pictures, trying to match their insect as closely as possible to those shown. If you are uncertain, it is wise to check if the individual is a dragonfly or damselfly first (see Key opposite). It will be possible to identify most species or groups of species from the photographs, combined with the descriptions. In many cases, though, this will only lead you to a group, e.g. *Lestes*, or *Aeshna*, leaving uncertainty as to which species it is within the group. For all the difficult groups, a Key is provided which will allow identification. For those unfamiliar with their operation, you begin at question 1, and decide which set of characters given match your individual; this will then lead you either to another numbered question, or an answer. If you are directed to another question, continue as before, and so on until you reach the point where a species name is given. This should be the correct identification, which can then be cross-checked with the pictures, diagrams and text. If you have no idea what the species is, follow the Key to families (adults), and proceed once you have established which family your specimen is in.

In the descriptions of species, **flight period** is the time during which you are most likely to see the adults. A few may occur outside this period. Dragonflies tend to emerge earlier further south, and where the south of the area is markedly different from the UK, the difference is specified. There will also be seasonal variations. The **description** concentrates on features that will aid identification. Teneral males usually resemble females in colouring. The **similar species** section endeavours to suggest species that might be confused, and key differences are given. It is wise to check all these species if you are uncertain of the first identification. The **habitat** given is the type of locality where the adults most frequently occur. Only the larvae are tied precisely to the habitat, and adults may wander considerably, though most individuals are found close to where they emerged or are likely to lay eggs. Habitat preferences vary through the area, and any clear differences are described. The **status and distribution** gives the degree of rarity or abundance of the species in a generalised way, indicating variations through the range where relevant. The broad distribution of the species is given, with more detail for the UK. Species continue to be found in new areas, so an identification cannot be ruled out on the grounds of distribution alone, but species (other than migratory ones) in totally new areas are highly unlikely. Species not known to occur in the UK are marked with an asterisk, thus *.

A Key to the families of Odonata adults

Many of the primary characteristics on which the differences between families are based are those associated with the pattern of wing venation. These are complex, and, in most cases, particularly diffcult to apply in the field even with a captive insect. The emphasis in this Key is on characteristics which can be seen reasonably easily on a captive insect in the field. It is, in fact, rare that one needs to proceed to work out the family of an insect before being able to identify it; it is much more likely that the individual will be roughly or exactly matched with the photographs and diagrams, and then precisely identified with the detailed Keys or descriptions.

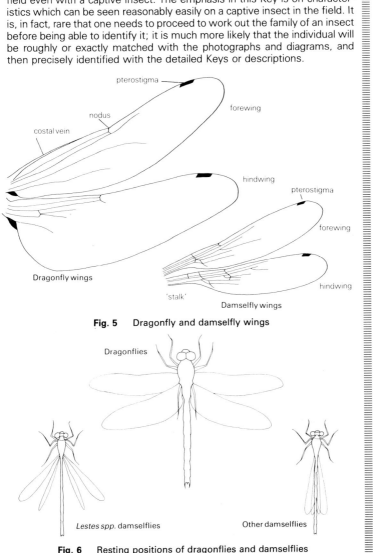

Fig. 5 Dragonfly and damselfly wings

Fig. 6 Resting positions of dragonflies and damselflies

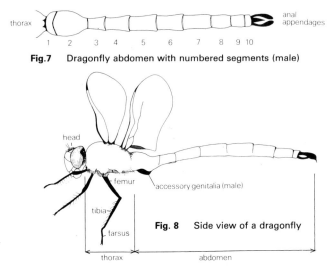

Fig.7 Dragonfly abdomen with numbered segments (male)

Fig. 8 Side view of a dragonfly

1   Fore- and hindwings similar in shape. Eyes always widely separated from each other, projecting markedly at the sides of the head; wings held back along the length of the abdomen when at rest (except in *Lestes* which often holds them half open, see fig. 6). Males with two superior and two inferior appendages. Generally delicate insects with weak flight   Damselflies ZYGOPTERA **2**

— Fore- and hindwings different in shape, with hindwings much broader at base; wings held more or less at right angles to body when at rest; eyes usually touching at some point (except in the family Gomphidae). Males with two superior and one inferior anal appendages. Generally large and strong-flying insects   Dragonflies ANISOPTERA **5**

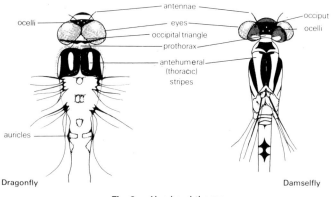

Fig. 9   Head and thorax

ZYGOPTERA   The Damselflies

2   Wings heavily suffused with colour, without 'stalks' at base. No pterostigma in male, false clear one in female. Body metallic blue or green   Calopterygidae (formerly Agriidae) (*Calopteryx*) (page 52)

—   Wings clear and with distinct narrowed 'stalks'. Pterostigmas present in male and female   **3**

3   Body metallic green (and one species dull-brown) and outer anal appendages prominent and clasper-like (see fig. 11)   Lestidae (page 54)

—   Not as above   **4**

4   Hind tibiae of males (see fig. 12) flattened and feathered, very pale Platycnemididae (*Platycnemis*) (page 63)

—   Legs not flattened and feathered as above, not white in mature individuals   Coenagrioniidae (page 70)

Fig. 10   Damselfly (*Enallagma spp.*) anal appendages   **Fig. 11**   *Lestes sponsa* anal appendages   **Fig. 12**   Enlarged tibia of *Platycnemis pennipes*

ANISOPTERA   The Dragonflies

5   Eyes widely separated (see fig. 13)   Gomphidae (page 84)

—   Eyes touching, even if only just   **6**

6   Eyes only just touching at one point (see fig. 14). Large species with black abdomens ringed with yellow: female with long pointed ovipositor   Cordulegasteridae (*Cordulegaster*) (page 108)

—   Eyes touching at more than just one point. Not as above   **7**

7   Metallic dark green species (except *Epitheca bimaculata** which is brown, black and yellow with a clubbed abdomen); eyes with a distinct tooth and indentation in the middle of the posterior edge (see fig. 15); auricles present on second abdominal segment of male (see fig. 16) Corduliidae (page 110)

—   Hind edge of eyes not toothed; combination not as above   **8**

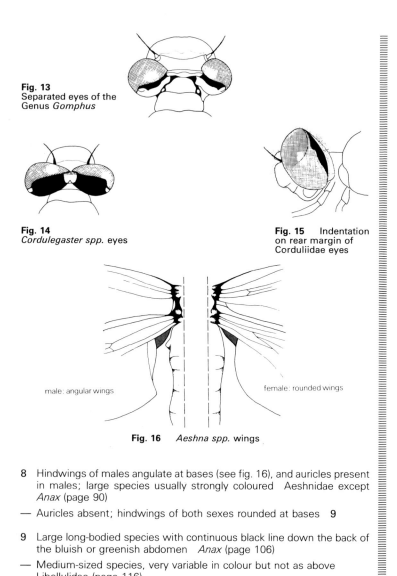

Fig. 13
Separated eyes of the
Genus *Gomphus*

Fig. 14
Cordulegaster spp. eyes

Fig. 15 Indentation
on rear margin of
Corduliidae eyes

male: angular wings

female: rounded wings

Fig. 16 *Aeshna spp.* wings

8   Hindwings of males angulate at bases (see fig. 16), and auricles present
    in males; large species usually strongly coloured   Aeshnidae except
    Anax (page 90)

—   Auricles absent; hindwings of both sexes rounded at bases   **9**

9   Large long-bodied species with continuous black line down the back of
    the bluish or greenish abdomen   *Anax* (page 106)

—   Medium-sized species, very variable in colour but not as above
    Libellulidae (page 116)

Finding and identifying larvae of dragonflies

Larvae can be searched for at any time of the year, although they are more easily found in warm weather. A standard pond net *with a strong frame* is suitable, and a long handle is useful if the whole structure is strong enough. A line and hook(s) for pulling in weed may reveal different species. The 'catch' will then need to be placed on a sheet of polythene or in a large white tray, and examined carefully. Many species will lie still for a short period, so observe the dèbris closely for a while before discarding it. Some experienced larva collectors find a 5 mm sieve, of the garden type, very useful for sorting out unwanted material and rapidly removing water. Any larvae collected should then be placed in water-filled containers with some weed, and carefully labelled with habitat, locality and date. Any unwanted material should be returned to the water, and no more material than you can deal with should be collected. You should ensure that you have facilities for keeping the larvae, before you collect them, if you intend to rear any. Moving water species are particularly difficult to keep.

Exuviae can also be collected, and of course this can do no harm at all to the population. They have to be collected soon after emergence as they deteriorate outdoors quite quickly. If you find an adult emerging, collect the exuvia afterwards since you will be more sure of its identification and can keep it as a reference. Details of the position and habitat of the exuvia should be noted, and it can be pinned to card or cork as part of a labelled reference collection at home.

A Key to families of Odonata larvae

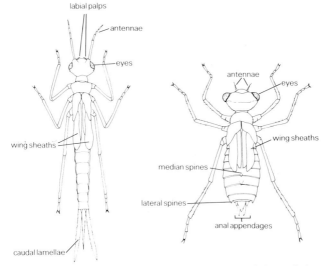

Fig. 17   A typical damselfly larva
(*Calopteryx virgo*)

Fig. 18   A typical dragonfly larva
(*Sympetrum danae*)

1 Larva long and slender, swimming by undulation. Abdomen terminating in three caudal lamellae (see fig. 17)   Damselflies ZYGOPTERA **2**

— Larva broader and more robust; abdomen without three lamellae, terminating in a number of short spiny appendages (see fig. 18). Swims in short bursts, through expulsion of water at rear end Dragonflies ANISOPTERA **5**

ZYGOPTERA   The Damselflies

2 Antennae with the first part as long as the remaining six together; middle lobe of mask (labium) with large deep cleft (see fig. 19). Caudal lamellae narrow   Calopterygidae (formerly Agriidae) (*Calopteryx*) (page 52)

— Antennae with the first part much shorter than the total length of the remaining six; labium with median cleft small or absent; caudal lamellae broad   **3**

3 Labial palps have a moveable hook with bristles; labium usually strongly contracted into a narrow base (see figs. 20 and 21); median cleft small and slit-like; caudal lamellae rounded at apex   Lestidae (page 54)

— Moveable hook on labial palps without bristles; labium not strongly contracted basally, more or less triangular overall; median slit absent, caudal lamellae often pointed at tips   **4**

4 Caudal lamellae with pronounced, very fine point; antennae with first segment shorter than pedicel; labial palps with bristles on outer margin   Platycnemididae (*Platycnemis*) (page 63)

— Antennae with first segment larger than pedicel; caudal lamella rounded or pointed, but lacking a pronounced fine point; labial palps without lateral bristles (except for *Coenagrion mercuriale* which has a few short bristles)   Coenagrioniidae (page 70)

Fig. 19   *Calopteryx virgo* labium with cleft

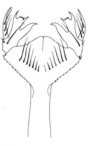

Fig. 20   *Lestes dryas* labium with strongly contracted base

Fig. 21   *Lestes spp.* moveable hook with bristles

ANISOPTERA The Dragonflies

5 Antennae composed of four broad segments, usually short; tarsi of hind legs with three segments, those of middle and front legs with two only; larvae often dorsiventrally flattened Gomphidae (page 84)

— Antennae composed of seven segments, all more or less long and thin; tarsi composed of three segments on all legs; larvae not dorsiventrally flattened 6

6 Mask flat, not rounded; inner margin of labial palps without teeth or bristles (see fig. 22); mobile hook well-developed; abdomen very long Aeshnidae (page 90)

— Mask curved, spoon-shaped; inner margin of labial palps toothed; palps and labium bristly; mobile hook poorly developed 7

7 Mask with bifid middle lobe, each point curved (see fig. 23); inner margin of palps strongly and irregularly toothed; abdomen long Cordulegasteridae (page 108)

— Mask without bifid middle lobe, inner margin of palps weakly toothed 8

8 Cerci distinctly more than half the length of paraprocts (see fig. 24); legs notably long; inner margin of labial palp with regular undulations (see fig. 25) Corduliidae (page 110)

— Cerci less than, or just equal to, length of paraprocts; legs generally short; (except *Sympetrum*), labial palp with inner margin with shallow or very reduced undulations (see fig. 26) Libellulidae (page 116)

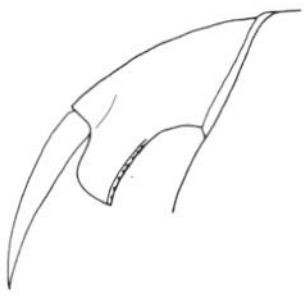

Fig. 22 *Aeshna spp.*
inner margin of labial palp

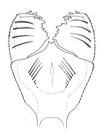

Fig. 23 *Cordulegaster spp.*
mask with bifid middle lobe

Fig. 24 Corduliidae cerci and paraprocts (*Oxygastra curtisii*)

cerci   paraprocts

Fig. 25
Somatochlora spp. (Corduliidae) inner margins of labial palp

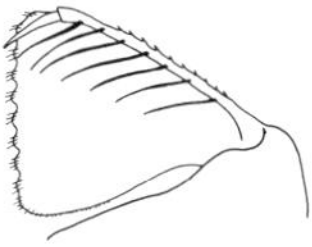

Fig. 26 *Libellula spp.* inner margin of labial palp

ORDER ODONATA: THE DAMSELFLIES AND DRAGONFLIES

Suborder Zygoptera The Damselflies

Family Calopterygidae

Genus *Calopteryx*

This family was formerly Agriidae with one genus *Agrion*. There are two similar species of this genus in the area. They are large damselflies with unusually broad, highly-coloured wings, and are occasionally mistaken for butterflies. The males have no pterostigmas, while the females have a false colourless pterostigma near the tip of each wing. The two males are readily distinguished though the females may be more difficult. Both are species of flowing waters.

Calopteryx virgo The Demoiselle Agrion

Size Abdomen length: 33–38 mm. Hindwing length: 28–34 mm. **Flight period** May to August, most abundant in June and July. **Description Males** The large, coloured wings distinguish this genus from all other damselflies. They have a bright metallic greenish-blue body, and wings suffused with brownish-blue almost to the tip, with no pterostigma. **Females** The body is metallic greenish-bronze to emerald green, with wings completely suffused with russet or purple-brown pigment. There is a false colourless pterostigma on each wing, larger on the forewing than hindwing. **Similar species** Only *C. splendens* is similar. Males of *C. splendens* have markedly banded wings of blue on a brownish ground colour, and their bodies are bluer. Females of *C. splendens* are more similar, but their wings are usually green rather than russet, and their abdomen is usually greener. There is usually a habitat distinction too. **Habitat** This species breeds almost entirely in flowing water, with a strong preference for faster, clearer, more acid waters than *C. splendens*. Most good sites are acid–neutral, unpolluted streams, with abundant aquatic vegetation, some shady areas, and a gravel or sand base. Adults stay close to their larval habitat, though they may occasionally occur elsewhere. **Behaviour** The mature males of the genus *Calopteryx* have a fascinating behaviour exhibiting both territorial defence and courtship; *C. virgo* behaviour is similar to that of *C. splendens*, described fully under that species. Females are less active and settle readily on marginal vegetation. Eggs are laid into plant tissue, and sometimes the females are observed submerging to achieve this. **Larval stages** The larvae live close to, or on the base of flowing water, often amongst stones or debris or amongst vegetation. Their development to the adult stage takes two or three years, with little synchronisation of emergence. Feeding takes place at night. Length of largest instars about 30 mm. **Status and distribution** Primarily a southern and western species in Britain, most abundant in the New Forest and Cornwall; it is absent from much of north and east Britain and declining in many lowland agricultural areas. On the continent, it is spread throughout the area, but always local and in decline in all the more intensively used areas.

▲ *Calopteryx virgo* ♂

▼ *Calopteryx virgo* ♀

Calopteryx splendens The Banded Agrion

Size Abdomen length: 34–40 mm. Hindwing length: 31 mm. **Flight period** May to September, most readily seen in June and July. **Description   Males** are one of the most beautiful of our insects, characterised by a strongly-coloured almost circular deep blue patch on the middle of each wing (or towards the tips in *subspp. caprai*) giving the impression of flickering bands when in flight. The body is metallic blue in adult males, with a greenish tinge towards the tip of the abdomen and along the sides of the thorax.   **Females** and teneral males, have a metallic green body later becoming bronzed in older females. The wings are suffused with green, except for the small white false pterostigmas. **Similar species** Only *C. virgo* (see under *C. virgo* for distinctions). *C. xanthostoma* has wing patches at the tip of the wings, and is yellow (not white) under the tip of the male's abdomen. **Habitat** Almost always associated with slower-moving depositional lowland streams and canals. Although it tolerates some silt load in the water, it is less likely to be found in polluted or very muddy water, and it needs abundant emergent vegetation, and plenty of sunny areas. The favoured habitats are meandering unimproved rivers in meadowland, though such situations are becoming rare. It also breeds in still water occasionally. **Behaviour** This is a very conspicuous species, often the first Odonata representative to be noticed by naturalists. It is usually abundant where it does occur, and the males are much more in evidence, flying out over the water, displaying, courting or perching visibly on water lilies or other vegetation, with sometimes up to five or six together. The females are less obvious but are usually close-by and readily found. The courtship dance in which the male flutters in front of the female, before leading her to the egg-laying site, is well-known and often observed. The male defends a distinct territory which will include perches, shelter and egg-laying sites, and from which other males are vigorously excluded. **Larval stages** The larvae live amongst water weeds and debris, usually close to the bottom mud, in streams and rivers. They are about 30 mm long, usually brown but sometimes grey or green, and are more readily found than *C. virgo* larvae. **Status and distribution** In Britain, this is primarily a southern species, widespread in the south and midlands, but rare or absent from Scotland and the north. Although declining, it is still locally common and may be abundant in favoured sites. It is widespread and locally frequent through Europe, as far north as southern Scandinavia but declining as a result of pollution and changes in river management.

Family Lestidae

Genera *Sympecma* and *Lestes*

A small family comprising, in N. Europe, one species of the genus *Sympecma*, and five species of *Lestes*. The genus *Sympecma* is unique in Europe in that the adults overwinter. The *Lestes* species can be very difficult to separate on field characteristics, and it is suggested that as many characters as possible are used before identification is certain. For the rarer species (e.g. *L. dryas* in Britain) new records will probably not be accepted without a specimen. Only *L. sponsa* and *L. dryas* (with *L. barbarus* and *L. viridis* in the Channel Islands) occur in Britain, but all five can occur in the remainder of the area, and habitat separation is not distinctive. *Lestes* species as a group usually hold their wings away from the body at about 45° when at rest, unlike most other damselflies.

▲ *Calopteryx splendens* ♂   ▼ *Calopteryx splendens* ♀

Sympecma fusca

Size Abdomen length 27–29 mm. Hindwing length: 20–22 mm. **Flight period** July to late May; sporadically in winter during warm weather. **Description** Generally dull brown or very dark after hibernation. **Males** have thorax brown or greenish above with cream stripes on sides; abdomen dark brown with cream markings, darkening with age. The pterostigmas are at different places on the fore- and hindwings, and this is readily visible at rest. Anal appendages clasper-like, pale reddish. **Females** are similar, anal appendages short and straight. **Similar species** Could be confused at first with aged individuals of *Lestes*, *Ischnura* and other damselflies. The flight period, and the pterostigmas in different positions are useful guides. **Habitat** They breed in a wide variety of still waters of about neutral pH, and may occur in brackish water. The adults move well away in autumn and winter, and are often seen in woods, scrub and other sheltered habitats. **Behaviour** Notable as the only European genus that overwinters as an adult. The adults leave their breeding sites in autumn and find sheltered hibernation sites under leaves, in hollow trees, wood-piles etc, from which they emerge in warm winter days, and finally emerge fully in March. They perch frequently with wings closed along the body (unlike *Lestes*) often on supports that are the same colour as themselves. Egg-laying takes place in tandem, with the eggs laid into water plants or floating debris. **Larval stages** The larvae are active bottom-dwellers, moving rapidly, and developing very quickly, taking a total of about two months. **Status and distribution** Not in UK, though recorded in Jersey. Elsewhere they are widespread and common throughout N. Europe as far north as Denmark.

Key to species of the genus *Lestes*

1   Abdomen long (33–40 mm). dark metallic green, with distinctive white or cream claspers in male, and pterostigma very pale brown or cream with *black* edges   *L. viridis** (page 60)

—   Abdomen shorter (25–32 mm) often more yellowish-green sometimes with blue patches, claspers not white, and pterostigmas with pale or blurred edges, or bicoloured   **2**

2   Pterostigma distinctively bicoloured brown nearest to the body, creamy towards the wing tip, back of head yellow; and appendages yellowish, tipped dark in males   *L. barbarus** (page 58)

—   Pterostigma single-coloured, though frequently edged laterally with pale lines   **3**

3   The remaining three species are readily confused, especially if aged or very young individuals are examined. The Key should be used in conjunction with figs. 27–29.

—   Pterostigma pale brown always bordered with pale stripes, back of head with broad yellow stripes between prothorax and êyes on both sides; anal appendages pale brown in both sexes   *L. virens** (page 58)

—   Pterostigmas darker, though sometimes edged with pale; back of head greenish or bluish, anal appendages black   **4**

Sympecma fusca ♂

Fig. 27 *Lestes dryas* anal appendages

Fig. 28 *Lestes sponsa* anal appendages

Lestes dryas female

Lestes sponsa female

Fig. 29 Markings on segment one

4   Pterostigma at least three times as long as broad in males, (about 3:1 in females), metallic marking on segment one of females rounded at top corners (similar in males but hard to see); (see fig. 29) females with slender abdomen, almost as narrow as males; segment two of male abdomen usually all blue; anal appendages as shown (see fig. 28) *L. sponsa* (page 60)

—   Pterostigma shorter and squarer, just over twice as long as broad; marking on segment one of females square at top corners (see fig. 29); ovipositor much more robust than in *L. sponsa*; female abdomen much more robust than males; segment two of male abdomen usually blue above green below (not 100% reliable), and appendages as shown (see fig. 27). Rare species in UK   *L. dryas* (page 62)

Lestes barbarus *

Size Abdomen length: 28–32 mm. Hindwing length: 20–25 mm. **Flight period** Late May to mid-September. **Description** A distinctive species by virtue of the bicoloured pterostigmas (brownish at the near end, cream beyond), the bright yellow back to the head, and the pale anal appendages. Otherwise very similar to other *Lestes* though lacking any marked blue colour in either sex. **Similar species** Other *Lestes* are generally similar, but mature individuals can easily be identified from the characters given. **Habitat** Occurs in a wide variety of acid–neutral, and occasionally brackish wetlands, such as lakes, marshes and bogs. The sites usually have abundant emergent vegetation. **Behaviour** Very similar to *L. sponsa* and others, though more likely to move away from water than *sponsa* and *dryas*, often found well away from breeding sites. **Larval stages** Exactly analogous with *L. sponsa*. **Status and distribution** Not in UK. Primarily southern, rare in the north and prone to temporary colonisation followed by extinction; not uncommon in the south of the area.

Lestes virens *

Size Abdomen length: 25–30 mm. Hindwing length: 18–22 mm. **Flight period** End of June to September or early October. **Description** Rather similar to *L. sponsa*, but with distinctive yellow stripes on the back of the head, a pale brown pterostigma bordered laterally with white, pale (not black) anal appendages, and, usually, rather less blue in the males. Females are a little less robust than *L. dryas*. In N. Europe, most individuals are referable to *subssp. vestalis*, distinguished from the type by the lateral thoracic yellow stripe being interrupted by a greenish patch at the distal end. **Similar species** Particularly similar to *L. dryas* and *L. sponsa* but a specimen in the hand (or in a clear photograph) can be distinguished by the characters given in the key, and above. **Habitat** A wide range of still waters, including lakes, ponds, marshes and ditches, usually well-vegetated. Occasionally in bogs. **Behaviour** Very similar to *L. sponsa* in behaviour. **Larval stages** Weed-dwellers, very similar to *L. sponsa*, taking 2–3 months to develop. **Status and distribution** Occurs throughout the area, as far north as Denmark. Widespread and frequent, though rather less common than *L. sponsa*. Not found in UK.

Lestes barbarus
♀

Lestes virens
♂

Lestes virens
♀

Lestes viridis* (syn. Chalcolestes viridis)

Size Abdomen length: 32–40 mm. Hindwing length: 24–28 mm. **Flight period** Late June to November. **Description** Bronze-green, but usually darker than other *Lestes* species, with a distinctly longer abdomen in comparison. The green colour may become bluish, but not bright blue. The anal appendages are almost white, and are conspicuous in the male. The pterostigmas are pale, white to pale brown, surrounded with black nerves. The back of the head is green or blue-green, not bright yellow. **Similar species** Only other *Lestes*, from which *L. viridis* is quite distinct. **Habitat** Occurs in a wide variety of still waters, but is also the most frequent *Lestes* in flowing waters. It is a wide-ranging species, and can be found anywhere in its area. **Behaviour** Broadly similar to other *Lestes* except for the distinctive egg-laying behaviour. Eggs are laid by the females, usually still paired, into the bark of trees and shrubs (of various species) close to the water. Two or three eggs are inserted at each point, and these frequently cause local swelling or gall formation, and may even cause significant damage. When the prolarvae hatch, they fall off and find their way to water before moulting. **Larval stages** They are mud and debris-dwellers, similar to other *Lestes*, and take 2–3 months to develop. **Status and distribution** Not in UK. Common and widespread throughout the south of the area, becoming rarer northwards as far as Denmark.

Lestes sponsa   The Emerald Damselfly

Size Abdomen length: 26–32 mm. Hindwing length: 19–23 mm. **Flight period** June to September (or even early November in warmer localities). **Description** Both sexes predominantly metallic green; wings are held partly away from the body at rest.   **Males** Head, thorax and abdomen basically metallic green, but with prothorax, and segments 1–2 and 9–10 of abdomen blue. Eyes blue. Pterostigma pale brown or dark brown, a little more than three times as long as broad. Anal appendages as in fig. 28, black in colour. **Females** Very similar except usually lacking blue colour. Top of markings on segment 9 rounded (see fig. 29). Pterostigma slightly squatter than those of male. Anal appendages short and straight. **Similar species** Other *Lestes*, especially *L. dryas* and *L. virens*.* See key for distinctions. **Habitat** A species of wide tolerances, occuring in almost all forms of still, or slow-moving water especially if sheltered and with good marginal vegetation. Tolerates quite acid water, and will also breed in brackish sites. Remains close to larval habitat usually. **Behaviour** A rather passive species, without notable characteristics. Both sexes remain close to emergent vegetation, rarely going far over water, and settling frequently. Egg-laying takes place as a pair, with the female laying into emergent or floating plants, often submerging totally for up to 30 minutes. Adults usually do not move far from their breeding sites. **Larval stages** Overwinters as an egg, and larval development thereafter is rapid, taking about 8–10 weeks. The larva is an active weed-dweller, about 25 mm long. **Status and distribution** Common and widespread throughout Britain almost where-ever there are suitable habitats. Absent from some seemingly suitable habitats, but frequently abundant where it does occur. It is common and widespread throughout the whole of the area.

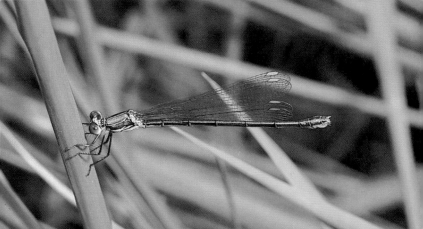

Lestes viridis
♂
(top)

Lestes viridis
♀
(centre)

Lestes sponsa
♂

Lestes dryas ♂

Lestes dryas   The Scarce Emerald Damselfly

Size Abdomen length: 28–32 mm. Hindwing length: 20–25 mm. **Flight period** Mid-June to October, slightly later than *L. sponsa* in similar latitudes. **Decription   Males** are exactly as *L. sponsa* except for the squarer (but barely visible) segment one markings, the bicoloured blue and green segment two (not a very reliable distinction), the slightly different anal appendages (see fig. 27), and the rather squarer pterostigma (less than three times as long as broad). **Females** have much more robust abdomen than males, and than *L. sponsa* females; segment one markings with square tops (see fig. 29); pterostigmas as males. **Similar species** Mainly *L. sponsa* and *L. virens*.* See key for distinctions. **Habitat** Very restricted in Britain, occurring almost entirely in shallow well-vegetated ditches, usually near the coast and occasionally brackish. Also occurs in suitable warm shallow ponds in similar sites. In N. Europe, it is much more tolerant, occurring in bogs, ditches and lakes, usually slightly to moderately acid. **Behaviour** Very similar to *L. sponsa* although, if anything, more inconspicuous. Tends to lay eggs above the water level, on plants. **Larval stages** Very similar to those of *L. sponsa*, with a similar or slightly faster development time, perhaps because they occur in warmer shallower water. **Status and distribution** Recently thought to have become extinct in UK, but rediscovered in 1983 and subsequently found in a number of coastal sites in south-east England. It is uncertain whether this is as a result of recolonisation from the continent, or because it had been overlooked. On the continent, it is as widespread as *L. sponsa*, but rather less common, and rarely abundant in a site.

Lestes dryas ♀

Family Platycnemididae
Genus *Platycnemis*

Represented in Europe only by the distinctive genus *Platycnemis* of which two species occur in the area. Both species have markedly swollen tibiae in the males, readily visible in the field, as do *P. pennipes* females.

Paired *Platycnemis pennipes*

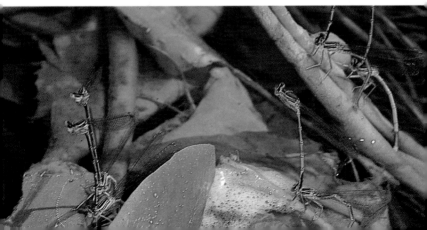

Platycnemis pennipes The White-legged Damselfly

Size: Abdomen length: 27–31 mm. Hindwing length: 19–23 mm. **Flight period** Late May to mid-August in UK, a little longer in Europe. **Description** A pale and rather delicate species. Both sexes have distinctive enlarged white hind tibiae. **Males** are pale blue with a black line extending dorsally through all segments, broadening into a black 'tail' on the last four segments. The base colour varies from white through green to quite dark blue. **Females** are similar to males but greenish-yellow (or occasionally white) and lacking the distinct black abdomen tip. **Similar species** Readily distinguished from other blue damselflies by the enlarged tibias. *P. acutipennis** is orange in the males, and the females do not have dilated legs. *P. latipes** occurs in the south of the area, and can be distinguished by the lack of a black line on the tibiae, the lack of a black line on segments 1–5 of the abdomen, and a distinctly white colour even when mature. **Habitat** In Britain, this is a species of unpolluted, well-vegetated, slow-moving rivers and streams, very similar to *C. splendens* in requirements. In Europe, it is more catholic and can occur in most water bodies, but especially slow-moving ones. **Behaviour** There is a short courtship display before mating, in which the males dangle their enlarged white legs in front of the female, and then grasp the females in flight (unlike many demselflies). The females lay into water plants, but usually remain above water themselves while doing so. Males, particularly, may fly up high when disturbed. **Larval stages** Slow-moving bottom-dwellers, usually found in or amongst mud, taking 1–2 years to develop. Length about 20 mm. **Status and distribution** A rather local southern species in the UK, affected by pollution and probably declining in some areas. In continental Europe it is both more common and widespread throughout the area, and is frequently abundant.

*Platycnemis acutipennis**

Size Abdomen length: 25–28 mm. Hindwing length: 18–19 mm. **Flight period** Late May to July. **Description** **Males** are a non-metallic orange, with bluish eyes and pale legs, expanded as in *P. pennipes* with a similar black line. **Females** are pale orange or cream, with barely dilated tibia. **Similar species** Males are very distinctive. See *P. pennipes* for other distinctions. **Habitat** Slow-moving waters, especially canals and lowland rivers, though occasionally in still water. Often occurs with *P. pennipes*. **Behaviour** Broadly similar to *P. pennipes*. **Larval stages** As *P. pennipes*. **Status and distribution** Not in UK. Locally abundant in suitable habitats throughout most of France, especially further south, but absent from the remainder of the area.

▲ *Platycnemis pennipes* ♂   ▼ *Platycnemis acutipennis* ♂

Family Coenagrioniidae

Genera *Pyrrhosoma* and *Ceriagrion*
The Red Damselflies

There are two species of red damselflies within the area, both in the Coenagrioniidae, but in different genera. They are brought together here since they are often confused by the beginner.

Pyrrhosoma nymphula   The Large Red Damselfly

Size Abdomen 25–29 mm. Hindwing length: 19–24 mm. **Flight period** Late April to early September. **Description** A robust species rather variable in colour. **Males** are predominately red, although with black legs, thorax black striped red, and segments 7–9 mainly black. Young males have yellow-green in place of red. **Females** are similar, though more robust and with a fine black line and patterns dorsally along the abdomen. **Similar species** Only *Ceriagrion tenellum* (below) is likely to be confused. This is smaller and slenderer, has red legs, thoracic stripes thin or absent, and a less hairy face. In the UK, it occurs in more acid habitats and is much rarer. See also *Platycnemis acutipennis**, page 64. **Habitat** Extremely catholic, occurring in most types of wetland, including brackish water and bogs, but not in fast-flowing rivers. **Behaviour** Not exceptional. A slow-moving species, readily approached and photographed. Egg-laying takes place in tandem, and the female may sometimes submerge wholly, taking the male with her. The young adults disperse widely into other habitats before they are reproductively mature. It is always one of the first species to emerge in spring. **Larval stages** A dark brown bottom-dweller amongst debris or submerged weeds, taking 1–2 years to mature. Length about 20 mm. **Status and distribution** Widespread and abundant in all wetland habitats throughout the area including the north, and in mountain areas up to at least 1400 metres. Probably the commonest damselfly in the region.

Ceriagrion tenellum   The Small Red Damselfly

Size Abdomen length: 23–28 mm. Hindwing length: 15–20 mm. **Flight period** Late May to early September, with a peak in June–July. **Description** A small, slender species. **Males** are almost entirely red, except for blackish thorax without stripes. Legs red. **Females** are variable in colour, but face, thorax and legs similar to males, except for pale thin thoracic stripes; abdomen usually red in segments 1–3, black in segments 4–8, then red or black at the tip. There are also wholly red and wholly black forms. **Similar species** Only *P. nymphula*. See that species for distinctions. **Habitat** An acid water species in the UK but not elsewhere, often associated with bogs, though occasionally found in fens with a similar structure. Prefers stable habitats, with established vegetation, and does not colonise new sites readily. **Behaviour** A delicate species with a weak fluttering flight, rarely moving far, and settling readily. Often caught by sundews that occur frequently in similar habitats. The female lays into plants in shallow water or bog, submerging if necessary while the male rises up vertically by fluttering strongly. The adults rarely move far from their larval habitat. **Larval stages** Little-known in detail. The larvae are about 17–18 mm long. **Status and distribution** A notable species in Britain, confined to the south and west, almost entirely in heathland areas. Locally in abundance in suitable areas such as the New Forest. More widespread in the area further south, but rare in the north and absent from Scandinavia.

Pyrrhosoma
nymphula
♂

▲ *Ceriagrion*
tenellum
♂

Paired
Ceriagrion
tenellum

Genus *Ischnura*

A genus represented by two distinctive 'blue-tailed' species in the area.

Ischnura elegans The Blue-tailed Damselfly

Size Abdomen length: 22–29 mm. Hindwing length: 15–20 mm. **Flight period** Mid-May to mid-September. **Description** **Males** are generally dark blue-black with very distinctive blue 'tail' (segment eight only) to abdomen; there are two blue thoracic stripes, and two blue eye-spots. The pterostigmas are very distinctive; they are in the form of a pointed oval, blue-black at the near end, white at the far end, on both wings. **Females** are generally similar to males but much more variable, with blue replaced by lilac, orange or brown in various named forms. The eighth segment is always clearly different from adjacent ones even if not blue. The pterostigmas are similar to the male's but the bi-coloration is less marked. The anal appendages are straight and not curved outwards as in the male. **Similar species** *I. pumilio* (below) is most similar. It is smaller and slenderer, has the blue 'tail' on segment nine and half of eight (not just eight) and has almost square slightly two-toned pterostigmas and the pterostigma is larger in the forewing than the hindwing. Male *Erythromma* (see pages 82–83) species have distinctive red eyes, no eye-spots and different pterostigmas. **Habitat** Very widespread in still and slow-moving waters, even if slightly brackish, and also in temporary and unstable waters. Can stand some degree of pollution, unlike most species. **Behaviour** Usually stays closer to marginal vegetation than other similar species, frequently settling on the vegetation, especially if paired. Males sometimes attempt to mate together. Females lay alone into aquatic vegetation and debris. **Larval stages** A weed-dwelling species, frequently encountered during pond-dipping. The larvae grow very fast, and may complete two generations each year further south. Length about 20 mm. **Status and distribution** Common and widespread throughout the area, though scarcer in the uplands and the far north. One of the most frequently encountered species.

Ischnura pumilio The Scarce Blue-tailed Damselfly

Size Abdomen length: 22–25 mm. Hindwing length: 14–18 mm. **Flight period** Early May to October (late May to September in UK). **Description** **Males** are very similar superficially to *I. elegans* but smaller, with square pterostigmas, and the blue patch on the abdomen extending over all of segment nine and part of eight (visible in the field, as the dividing line can be seen in the middle of the blue, whereas there is no line in *I. elegans*) and along the sides of ten. **Females** are variable, though never like the male. Either greenish wherever the male is blue, with segments 8–10 bronze-black, or orange-red over the head, thorax and segments 1–3 of the abdomen (i.e. extending further than the comparable form of *I. elegans*), bronze-black on the remainder, though segment ten may be orange. **Similar species** See *I. elegans* for differences. *Nehalennia speciosa* might be confused, but is even smaller, has no eye spots and a squarer single-coloured pterostigma. **Habitat** A restricted species of bog pools, seepages, slow-moving streams

Ischnura elegans ♂ (top)   *Ischnura pumilio* ♂

and shallow ponds in Britain. In Europe, the habitats are similar but also embrace gravel pits – even new ones – brackish water and quite large lakes. **Behaviour** A weak species, always flying low and slowly over the water, settling frequently. The female lays without the male, though he is usually close by. **Larval stages** Similar to *I. elegans*, but the nymph is smaller, and takes longer in development. **Status and distribution** A rare and local south-western species in the UK, mainly in Hants, Dorset, Cornwall and Pembrokeshire. In Europe, it is rather more common and widespread, locally abundant, but rare in the north and absent from most of Scandinavia.

Genus *Coenagrion*

The genus *Coenagrion* comprises the majority of 'blue' damselflies likely to be found in the area. They may conceivably be confused with *Enallagma* (one species only) or *Ischnura* (two species) at first, though these latter can be learnt and distinguished with practice. Within the genus, species separation may be much more difficult and in some cases an examination of the anal appendages or prothorax is required for confirmation. Photographs are rarely good enough for positive identification, partly because the wings often obscure many of the distinguishing marks, and partly because it is often necessary to look at the individual from more than one direction to be sure of its identification. A selection of photographs of more distinctive species is shown, together with line drawings of all the male abdomens opposite. Habitat distinctions may be useful for confirming identifications (see under individual species) but there is too much overlap for certainty. Males are less difficult than females to identify, but neither is easy. For rare or unexpected species, a specimen is essential for the acceptance of the record as certain.

Partial Key to the genus *Coenagrion* (males)

1 A species with no dorsal thoracic stripes (antehumeral stripes), a long, predominantly black, abdomen (see fig. 33b) and very long pincer-shaped anal claspers (see fig. 30). Now extinct in UK   *C. armatum* (page 76)

— Not as above   **2**

2 Thoracic stripes present (normally blue on black), but interrupted by black to form a dot and a stripe on each side. Abdomen as fig. 33c *C. pulchellum* (page 78)

— Thoracic stripes present and unbroken   **3**

3 A species of gently-flowing water, characterised by long yellowish pterostigmas, anal claspers longer than the tenth abdominal segment (see fig. 31), and an abdominal pattern as shown in fig. 32a. Not recorded in UK   *C. lindenii** (page 72)

— Not as above. The remaining five species are best distinguished by the abdominal markings as shown in figs. 32 and 33 and the features mentioned in the species descriptions. Variants do occur, especially in some species, and there may be differences throughout the geographical range of some species. Great care is therefore needed when identifying any unlikely species.

Fig. 30
Anal appendages of
Coenagrion armatum

Fig. 31
Anal appendages of
Coenagrion lindenii

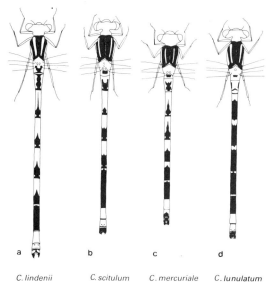

a   b   c   d

C. lindenii   *C. scitulum*   *C. mercuriale*   *C. lunulatum*

Fig. 32   *Coenagrion spp.* abdomen and thorax

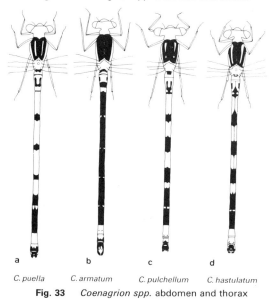

a   b   c   d

C. puella   *C. armatum*   *C. pulchellum*   *C. hastulatum*

Fig. 33   *Coenagrion spp.* abdomen and thorax

Coenagrion lindenii* (syn. *Cercion lindenii*)

Size Abdomen length: 25–30 mm. Hindwing length: 17–21 mm. **Flight period** Late April–May to August or early September. **Description Males** are a roughly equal mixture of blue and black, patterned as shown in fig. 32a. The anal appendages are distinctive, longer than segment ten (see fig. 31), and the pterostigma is yellow, rather longer and more pointed than in other species. **Females** are stoutly built, and may be green, bluish or creamy-yellow, with a black band of variable thickness along the length of the abdomen, dorsally. **Similar species** At a glance, this can be confused with most blue damselflies, but note its habitat and pay careful attention to the abdominal pattern and other features described in the Key. **Habitat** Principally a species of slow-moving waters such as canals, and lowland rivers, but also occurs in still waters, especially if these are along the course of a river, e.g. fishponds or reservoirs. Prefers sites with adequate emergent vegetation. **Behaviour** Not a particularly distinctive species. Egg-laying is readily observed: the male remains attached to the female while she lays, usually whilst above water, into aquatic plants (see page 18). If the female submerges, the male detaches and hovers over the egg-laying site until she re-appears. The adults usually remain close to their larval habitat, and may be quite abundant, often in company with *Platycnemis spp.* and *Calopteryx splendens*, though they are occasionally encountered well away from water. **Larval stages** The larvae are weed-dwellers, most frequently found amongst vegetation in the shallows of flowing water. Development seems to take place within one year, and the larvae emerge onto vertical stems for preference. **Status and distribution** A southern species within the area, absent from the UK, Denmark, and countries further north and rare in Holland and most of Germany. In the south of the area, especially in France, it is locally abundant in suitable habitats but is probably declining.

Coenagrion scitulum* The Dainty Damselfly

Size Abdomen length: 22–26 mm. Hindwing length: 15–20 mm. **Flight period** Late May to September (formerly June to July in UK where now presumed extinct). **Description** Male and female pale blue with black marking, and thoracic stripes present in both sexes (see fig. 32b). Both sexes have a long brownish pterostigma (about twice as long as deep) in contrast to other *Coenagrions* (except *C. lindenii*), where it is normally almost square. The markings on segment two of the abdomen varies from that shown from a stalked oval to a small unstalked dumbell shape. **Similar species** Similar to most of the smaller blue damselflies, especially *Coenagrion mercuriale* (see page 74) and *Enallagma cyathigera* (see page 80). The combination of abdominal pattern, long pterostigma and rather pointed thorax and prothorax is distinctive. **Habitat** In Britain, this species was only found around ponds and ditches near the coast in Essex, but elsewhere in the area it occurs in ponds, lakes, slow-moving rivers and even relatively rapid flowing streams. There is some association with sites containing water-milfoil *Myriophyllum*, but this is not consistent over the whole area. **Behaviour** Similar to most other *Coenagrions*. The adults remain close to their larval habitats through their life,

Coenagrion lindenii ♂ (top)   *Coenagrion scitulum* ♂ caught in a spider's web

and they tend to stay more out over open water than most species, perhaps because of competition from the larger blue damselflies. The epithet 'dainty' is apt, and the general impression is of a delicate insect, like *C. mercuriale*. **Larval stages** Little is known of this stage. They are weed-dwellers, and reach a length of about 15 mm before emerging. **Status and distribution** A southern species, absent from the UK, Denmark, most of Holland and Germany, and all countries further north. It is rare and local in the remainder of the region, and not abundant even where it does occur. It was known in the UK from 1946 to 1953, when a major sea flood destroyed its known sites, and it has not been seen since.

Coenagrion mercuriale   The Southern Damselfly

Size Abdomen length: 22–14 mm. Hindwing length: 15–18 mm. **Flight period** May to August. **Description** One of the smallest of the damselflies in the area, with only *I. pumilio* and *Nehalennia* smaller. This is noticeable in the field. **Males** are typically blue and black (see fig. 32c) with pronounced thoracic stripes, and two distinctive round blue 'eye-spots' joined by a blue line on the back of the head. The pterostigma in both sexes is very small, dark and diamond-shaped. The mercury mark on abdominal segment two is distinctive but not diagnostic in N. Europe. **Females** appear almost black from above, with a ground colour usually yellow to green, visible in the thoracic stripes, similar eye-spots, and bluish rings round the joints of segments 7–9. Old females may develop a blue ground colour. **Similar species** The males are generally similar to other blue damselflies, but smaller and more delicate; and the combination of mercury mark and general abdomen pattern, eye spots with bar and small pterostigma are reasonably diagnostic. **Habitat** In the UK it breeds in and around small streams associated with valley bogs, but only where there is a relatively high pH. It also occurs in chalk streams. There is a preference for areas with wet bare ground amongst vegetation, e.g. in flushed areas. Elsewhere, it occurs most often in flowing water, usually streams near their source, and normally calcareous. **Behaviour** Both males and females remain close to their breeding site. They fly slowly and low amongst well-vegetated areas, frequently perching on low vegetation. Eggs may be laid into wet mud or water, and the female may submerge entirely. The general impression of *C. mercuriale* is of a delicate insect. **Larval stages** The larvae are small, about 18 mm long, and live amongst weeds or in mud in shallow, flowing water. The life-cycle has not been studied in detail, but the larvae seem to develop over two years. **Status and distribution** A southern species, absent from north Germany and northwards, and the whole of the UK except the south-west. In the UK, it is rare, though locally common in the New Forest area and W. Wales. Elsewhere, it is never more than locally frequent even in the south of the area, probably because of its demanding habitat requirements.

Coenagrion lunulatum   The Irish Damselfly

Size Abdomen length: 23–26 mm. Hindwing length: 16–19 mm. **Flight period** June to July. **Description** A robust-looking species. **Males** are rather blacker in appearance than most *Coenagrions*, though segments eight and nine are clear blue. The 'digital U' mark on segment two is characteristic and not usually variable. **Females** heavily marked black on a blue, or sometimes green, base colour. The rear margin of the prothorax is three-lobed as in *C. pulchellum*. **Similar species** Could be confused with most blue damselflies. The second-segment mark on the males is usually definitive, and the three-lobed prothorax margin coupled with the clear blue segments eight and nine are key features. **Habitat** In the British Isles, known only in Ireland where it has been found in several bog and fen areas. Elsewhere, it occurs in acid boggy areas, including those in uplands, up to an altitude of about 1500 metres. **Behaviour** Similar to other *Coenagrion* species. **Larval stages** Broadly similar to other *Coenagrion* species. **Status and distribution** A rare species. Within the British Isles, known only from a few scattered sites in Ireland, all discovered since 1981. In Europe, it is a north-easterly and upland species, scattered very locally through Germany and Scandinavia. It is probably overlooked in places.

▲ *Coenagrion mercuriale* ♂

▼ *Coenagrion mercuriale* ♀

Coenagrion puella   The Azure Damselfly, The Common Coenagrion

Size Abdomen length: 23–30 mm. Hindwing length: 16–22 mm. **Flight period** Early May to early September. **Description   Males** predominantly blue with black markings of which the 'U' shape on segment two and the 'crown' on segment nine are most useful, though the 'U' in particular may vary. The blue thoracic stripes are uninterrupted. **Females** are mainly black on the dorsal surface, with yellow-green below, or occasionally blue. There is a heavy 'thistle-mark' on segment two. **Similar species** Similar to most blue damselflies, but most likely to be confused with *C. pulchellum* (see page 78) and *Enallagma cyathigera* (see page 80). Males of *C. pulchellum* normally have different abdominal markings especially on segments two and nine (see fig. 33c), and interrupted thoracic stripes while the females are much bluer than *puella*. For distinction from *Enallagma* see that species. **Habitat** Occurs in a wide variety of habitats, including ponds, lakes, canals, slow rivers, and ditches, especially where there is plenty of vegetation. Individuals will wander well away from water especially into lush meadowland. **Behaviour** Not a distinctive species. Both sexes fly low and settle readily on vegetation, both erect and floating. Both sexes leave water for a period and are often found in relatively dry habitats. Eggs are laid, while the pair is still in copulation, into plant tissue, and the female may submerge. **Larval stages** Weed-dwelling, and one of the most frequently found species when 'pond-dipping'. They may develop in less than a year. About 20–24 mm long. **Status and distribution** The commonest *Coenagrion* and frequently most abundant throughout the area except in the far north in Scotland and Denmark where it is rare or absent.

*Coenagrion armatum**   The Norfolk Damselfly

Size Abdomen length: 24–27 mm. Hindwing length: 17–20 mm. **Flight period** June to July. **Description** An unusually long-tailed species. **Males** are predominantly black, but segment two is mainly blue except for a spot and two black lines. Segments eight and nine are mainly blue. There are no dorsal thoracic stripes. The male appendages are noticeably long and pincer-like, diagnostic if seen magnified (see fig. 30). **Females** are less distinctive. Mainly black, but with segments one, two and eight mainly green dorsally, except for a pointed black spot on segment two. **Similar species** Normal fully-coloured males are quite distinctive, though might be taken for an *Ischnura* at first glance (see pages 68–69). Females could be confused with other *Coenagrion* females, though the mark on segment two, and the mainly green segment eight help to differentiate them. **Habitat** In Britain, this formerly occurred around several neutral lakes in the Norfolk Broads, though now believed extinct. In Europe it usually occurs in larger well-vegetated still water bodies, often in heathy areas, or occasionally in slow-moving waters. **Behaviour** Flies low but strongly over the water close to the banks, or amongst fringing vegetation such as reeds, settling readily on emergent or floating vegetation. **Larval stages** Little-studied. The larvae are weed-dwelling and about 25 mm long. **Status and distribution** A rare north-eastern species. Formerly known from the broads in Norfolk, but not seen there since 1957 due to pollution. The species is absent from the south and west of the area, rare in north Germany and Denmark, and slightly more frequent further north-east.

*Coenagrion
puella* ♂

*Coenagrion
puella* ♀

*Coenagrion
armatum* ♂

Coenagrion pulchellum   The Variable Damselfly

Size Abdomen length: 25–30 mm. Hindwing length: 16–21 mm. **Flight period** May to August, commonest in June to July. **Description** A notoriously variable species both in pattern and colour of the female. **Males** Medium sized blue and black species, with an abdomen as shown in fig. 33c. The second abdominal segment pattern and the interrupted and occasionally missing thoracic stripes are key features. The prothorax is prominently three-lobed where it joins the thorax. **Females** Commonly blue with many black markings, but may also be greenish or yellowish. The second segment bears a mercury mark. Thoracic stripes unbroken, but the prothorax is three-lobed as in the males. **Similar species** Similar to most blue damselflies, especially *C. puella* (see page 76) and *Enallagma cyathigera* (see page 80). Refer to those species for differences. The three-lobed prothorax of *C. pulchellum* is usually diagnostic. **Habitat** Prefers well-vegetated sites, often with little open water, such as fens, watermeadows, levels and marshes, or the margins of shallow ponds. May occur also in slow-flowing waters such as dykes or canals, if they are well-vegetated. **Behaviour** Generally similar to *C. puella*, though the adults of *pulchellum* are, if anything, even more prone to disperse into meadows and lanes, especially when immature. **Larval stages** As *C. puella* in size and habits: weed-dwelling. Development is complete in less than one year. **Status and distribution** Generally much less common and more restricted than *C. puella*, though nevertheless widespread. A noteworthy species in England and Wales and extremely rare in Scotland, but much commoner in mainland Europe, throughout the area, wherever suitable habitats exist, and especially common in south Scandinavia.

Coenagrion hastulatum   The Northern Damselfly

Size Abdomen length: 23–26 mm. Hindwing length: 17–22 mm. **Flight period** End of May to end of August. **Description** A typical medium-sized *Coenagrion*. **Males** are blue and black, with a distinctive marking on segment two consisting of a spearhead with two lines radiating from it (see fig. 33c). The spearhead varies but the lines are consistent. Segments eight and nine are clear blue. **Females** are predominantly black, with a greenish ventral ground colour. **Similar species** Most other blue damselflies similar, but especially likely to be confused with *C. lunulatum* (see page 74) and *Enallagma cyathigera* (see page 80) which can all occur together. Segment two of the males usually have different patterns; *C. lunulatum* has a more distinctly three-lobed prothorax, see *Enallagma* for distinction from that species. **Habitat** Almost always found in still, acid waters, usually with boggy margins containing *Sphagnum*, in upland and northern areas. **Behaviour** Similar to most *Coenagrion spp*. It is a rather passive species, which remains close to its larval habitat. **Larval stages** Little-known. They are probably much longer in development than lowland species. **Status and distribution** Very rare in Britain where it is confined to a few eastern Scottish sites. Absent from all the lowland parts in the south of the area, but quite common from Denmark northwards, and present in many alpine lakes.

*Coenagrion
pulchellum* ♂

*Coenagrion
pulchellum* ♀

*Coenagrion
hastulatum* ♂

Genus *Enallagma*

A genus of only one species in Europe, *E. cyathigera*. Despite its classification in a different genus, *E. cyathigera* is broadly similar to, and readily confused with, the remainder of the blue damselflies, in the field.

Enallagma cyathigera   The Common Blue Damselfly

Size Abdomen length: 24–28 mm. Hindwing length: 18–21 mm. **Flight period** Mid-May to early October. **Description** A robust species. Both sexes have pear-shaped blue 'eye-spots' joined by a bar, and only one, short, black line on the side of the thorax. **Males** are blue and black, with more blue than most species. The thorax has two broad blue dorsal stripes, abdominal segment two has a distinctive stalked 'ball', and both segments eight and nine are clear blue (except very occasionally marked on the eighth segment, see fig. 34). **Females** are mainly black-marked over a dull greenish or bluish colour, with two broad dorsal thoracic stripes, and a very distinctive spine vertically under segment eight, visible in the field. **Similar species** Readily confused with most 'blue' damselflies in the genus *Coenagrion*. *Enallagma* is separated by the single thin black line on the side of the thorax (see fig. 34) (cf. two in *Coenagrion spp.*) in both sexes. Male *Enallagma* have segments eight and nine all blue (only two *Coenagrion spp.* share this), the distinctive 'stalked ball' mark on segment two (not diagnostic as it varies towards that of *C. hastulatum*) and the generally bluer abdomen than most species. Females have the diagnostic spine below segment eight. The dorsal thoracic stripes are rather broader than in most *Coenagrion spp.* **Habitat** An adaptable species occurring in most types of wetland habitats, including brackish and slow-flowing waters, with a distinct preferences for large open waters with well-vegetated margins. It also occurs in mountain lakes and wetlands. **Behaviour** Notable as one of the most aggressive damselflies, with males attacking both other *Enallagma* males and those of other species. Several males may join forces to drive away other species. The bright blue males can often be seen flying strongly in 'swarms' low over the water surface well away from the edge, though most mating and territorial activity takes place on the margins where there are perches. The females habitually submerge for egg-laying, for as long as an hour, usually leaving the male behind. Individuals, especially young males, wander far from water. **Larval stages** Not distinctive. A weed-dweller, frequently abundant, and about 22–24 mm long. **Status and distribution** Common and frequently abundant throughout the area. In many northern and upland sites, it is the only damselfly visible; this may make it very hard work looking for *C. hastulatum* or *C. lunulatum*!

Nehalennia speciosa *

This is the smallest European damselfly with an abdomen length of 20 mm, and a hindwing length of only 12–15 mm. It is like a tiny *Erythromma* (see following page), easily distinguished though by its small size. It is very rare, occurring only in Germany and Switzerland within the area, in well-vegetated marshes, lakes or boggy sites.

*Enallagma
cyathigera* ♂

Fig. 34
*Enallagma
cyathigera*
thorax and
abdomen
markings

*Enallagma
cyathigera* ♀

81

Genus *Erythromma*

A genus of two species in Europe, both characterised by bright red eyes. Only *E. najas* occurs in the UK.

Erythromma najas   The Red-eyed Damselfly

Size Abdomen length: 25–30 mm. Hindwing length: 19–24 mm. **Flight period** May to early September. **Description** A robust, strong-flying species. **Males** are generally dark greenish-black, but with bright red eyes and a blue-tipped (segments nine to ten) abdomen. No thoracic stripes. The face is hairy. **Females** are rather similar, slightly paler in all respects, without the blue tail, and with short pale thoracic stripes. **Similar species** *E. viridulum* is most similar; it is less obviously robust, and segment ten has a distinct black cross over the blue (see photograph and fig. 36). See also *Ischnura elegans* (page 68) for distinctions from that species. **Habitat** Has a preference for larger ponds and lakes with abundant floating vegetation, such as water-lilies and pond-weeds. Also occurs in slow-moving waters and in the calmer backwaters of major rivers such as the Loire. **Behaviour** A distinctive species, with a strong direct flight, especially in the males, though surprisingly readily driven off by more aggressive species like *Enallagma*. Well-known for its habit in the males, of resting on the floating leaves of aquatic plants, especially water-lilies and pondweeds, from which it makes periodic sorties, often returning to the same point. Mats of algae or debris are also used, and the males will often perch on surrounding shrubs especially if there is little floating vegetation. Females will move well away from water into meadows or other habitats. Egg-laying takes place in tandem, usually into lily leaves, and the females may submerge entirely, going down a flower stem, with or without a male, for long periods. When the egg-laying is finished, she floats back to the surface. **Larval stages** Very active weed-dwellers, with rapid development, usually within one year. Length about 30 mm. **Status and distribution** Locally common in England only south of the Wash. Rare or absent in the north and west. On mainland Europe, it is frequent throughout the area, including south Scandinavia, up to an altitude of about 1200 metres.

*Erythromma viridulum**

Size Abdomen length: 22–24 mm. Hindwing length: 16–20 mm. **Flight period** June to early September. **Description** Very similar to *E. najas* but distinctly smaller and more slender; the thorax has two pale indistinct stripes, segment ten has a black mark rather like an 'x' and the anal appendages differ as shown in fig. 36. **Similar species** More readily confused with an *Ischnura* (see page 68) since it is smaller than *E. najas*, but the red eyes, and longer extent of blue on the tail are clear distinctions. **Habitat** Broadly similar to *E. najas*, perhaps preferring smaller waters. **Behaviour** As *E. najas*, though less strong in flight. **Larval stages** As *E. najas*. **Status and distribution** Not in UK, though occurring throughout the southern part of the area as far north as N. Germany. A little less frequent than *E. najas*.

Erythromma najas ♂

Fig. 35
Erythromma najas
anal appendages

Fig. 36
*Erythromnma
viridulum*
anal appendages

*Erythromma
viridulum* ♂

Suborder Anisoptera
The Dragonflies Family Gomphidae
Genus *Gomphus*

A very distinctive family, represented by seven species from three genera in the area, though there is only one British species. The Gomphids are unique amongst European dragonflies (Anisoptera) in having widely separated eyes – in all the other Anisoptera, the eyes touch for at least a part of their length. The individual species are not particularly easy to identify, and it is important to observe the colour of the legs, the thoracic pattern, and the anal appendages of the males, and other minor features as described.

Key to the four species of the genus *Gomphus*

1 Legs entirely black almost to the top   *G. vulgatissimus* (below)

— Legs yellow or striped with black   **2**

2 Side of thorax with black stripes converging towards the front to form a distinct 'Y' shape (see fig. 37)   *G. flavipes** (page 86)

— No clear 'Y' shape on side of thorax   **3**

3 Abdomen not strongly 'clubbed' at tip in males or females; legs yellow with longitudinal black stripes; still water species widespread in south of area   *G. pulchellus** (page 86)

— Abdomen distinctly 'clubbed' in males at segments eight and nine; posterior tarsi black. A southern species of flowing water, that barely reaches the area and is rare   *G. simillimus** (page 86)

Fig. 37   *Gomphus flavipes* showing Y-shape marking on thorax

Gomphus vulgatissimus   The Club-tailed Dragonfly

Size Abdomen length: 33–37 mm. Wingspan: 64 mm. **Flight period** Mid-May to end of June in UK, and from early May to early August elsewhere. **Description** A medium-sized, strongly marked species. **Males** are black with heavy yellowish-green markings and yellow on segments 8–10. The base of the hindwing looks 'cut'. Segments eight and nine of abdomen markedly expanded into the club-tail and narrowed at segments two to three. **Female** coloration generally similar, but abdomen thicker throughout and barely club-tailed; hindwing base rounded. **Similar species** Quite distinctive in UK. Readily confused with other European Gomphids, though the black legs and pattern of markings distinguish it satisfactorily. **Habitat** In Britain, this is entirely a species of flowing water, usually large river systems. It seems to be able to stand some pollution, though it has disappeared from some former sites. In Europe it normally occurs in rivers, but may breed in lakes

*Gomphus
vulgatissimus
♂*

*Gomphus
vulgatissimus
♀*

occasionally. **Behaviour** Distinctly sluggish for a dragonfly. They fly slowly, frequently hovering and settling readily, usually on vegetation, but also on stones, often for long periods. Rarely seen as more than one or two individuals. Males remain near water while the females are usually found away from water. Mating pairs often fly up into the trees, and then separate for the female to lay eggs alone. These are extruded in a gelatinous mass, to be knocked off when the female hits the surface of the water with her abdomen, over shallow areas. **Larval stages** Specialised mud-dwellers; they are very sluggish and lie partially-buried in the river mud, and are not often found. Development seems to take three to four years, possibly longer in the north. The larvae usually adopt a horizontal position for the adults to emerge, often on the bank. **Status and distribution** A very local southern species in England though locally abundant sometimes, e.g. on the River Thames and River Severn. Always worth noting. In Europe it is widespread throughout the area and by no means rare, though unlikely to be seen by the casual observer.

Gomphus pulchellus*

Size Abdomen length: 34—38 mm. Wingspan about 60 mm. **Flight period** May to late July. **Description** A slender rather weak species. **Males** are rather pale green-yellow marked with black; legs striped yellow and black. Abdomen not distinctly clubbed at tip; eyes blue-green, face yellow; hindwing bases look 'cut'. **Females** are very similar, with slightly stouter body and rounded hindwing bases. **Similar species** Identifiable as a Gomphid by separated eyes, though unusual in being found mainly in lakes. *G. simillimus** is very similar (see Key, page 48), but prefers flowing water, and barely reaches the area from the south. **Habitat** A species of lakes, fish-ponds, canals and the calmer parts of rivers, and occasionally in small streams. **Behaviour** Has a rather weak flight, reminiscent of an old *Sympetrum*, settling readily on the ground (particularly) or on vegetation. The females lay separately after mating, apparently scattering their eggs at random. **Larval stages** barely-known, though presumably broadly similar to the river Gomphids. **Status and distribution** Probably the most frequently encountered Gomphid in the south of the area. Rare in N. and E. Germany, and absent from the north of the area. Absent from the UK.

Gomphus simillimus*

Very similar in virtually all respects to *G. pulchellus**, and just occurs in the south of the area. It is distinguishable by the features shown in the Key (see page 84), but a close look is usually necessary. It occurs only in flowing waters, in southern Europe.

Gomphus flavipes*

An uncommon eastern species, occasionally found as far west as Holland and north France. It is similar to *G. vulgatissimus* but the legs are black and yellow striped (not black) and the abdomen is less clubbed. It occurs in large river systems and canals, settling frequently on sand-banks, rocks or the ground.

Genus *Ophiogomphus**

A genus of one species in the area, broadly similar to other Gomphids but distinguishable particularly by the wing-like projections on the male abdomen, segments seven to nine, and the two distinctive yellow horns with black tips on the head of the female (see fig. 38).

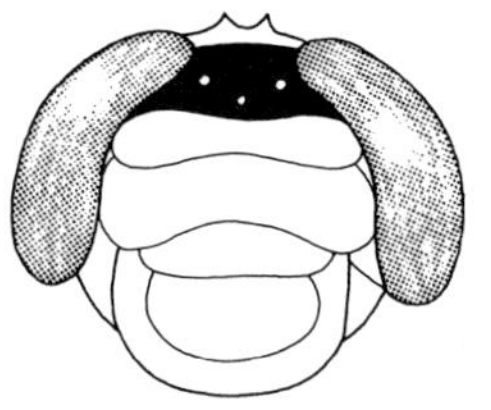

Fig. 38 Female *Ophiogomphus spp.* showing head with horns

▲ *Gomphus pulchellus* ♂   ▼ *Gomphus pulchellus*

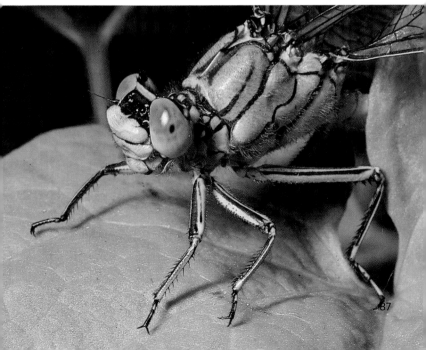

Ophiogomphus serpentinus*

Size Abdomen length: 37–39 mm. Wingspan: 64 mm. **Flight period** June to September. **Description** The general impression is similar to other Gomphids, but usually greenish rather than yellowish, with broad green stripes on the thorax, together with the distinctive features of the genus. **Similar species** Broadly similar to other Gomphids, but the 'winged' abdomen tip of the male, and the horns of the female are diagnostic, while the greenish colour will often provide an accurate quick identification. **Habitat** Flowing water, favouring faster-flowing rivers than most Gomphids, usually with sand or gravel banks. **Behaviour** A typical Gomphid, very similar to, for instance, *G. vulgatissimus* in habits. It flies little, and settles frequently, especially on warm ground – sandbanks, stones, roads, etc – or occasionally on vegetation. **Larval stages** Broadly similar to other Gomphids, though the larvae are more active and do not bury themselves so deeply in the mud. **Status and distribution** Not found in the UK. A rare species throughout the area, most likely to be found in the east, nearest to its centre of distribution in Asia.

Genus *Onychogomphus**

A genus of two species in the area, distinguishable by the combination of expanded abdomen tip and pincer-like anal appendages in the male, and the absence of 'horns' in the female.

Onychogomphus forcipatus*

Size Abdomen length: 32–38 mm. Wingspan: 60 mm. **Flight period** June to mid-September. **Description** A yellow and black insect. **Males** have a clubbed abdomen over segments seven to ten though less marked than *G. vulgatissimus*; the anal appendages are large and solid-looking, brown or brownish-yellow. **Females** are similar in coloration, with a thicker abdomen lacking the club-tail or pincer-like appendages. **Similar species** Rather similar to other Gomphids, but males distinguished from other genera by the anal appendages. *O. uncatus* is similar but has yellower anal appendages, the top of the head is plain black (cf. *O. forcipatus* has a tiny yellow spot there) and the eyes are blue (cf. green in *O. forcipatus*). *O. uncatus* only occurs on the southern edge of the area. **Habitat** Almost entirely a flowing water species, in streams, rivers or canals, and occasionally in lakes. It likes sites with sand banks or bare gravelly margins. **Behaviour** A typical Gomphid, spending much of its time settled on warm surfaces such as gravel banks or on rocks in the river, rarely settling on vegetation. It hardly ever flies far if disturbed, and soon settles again. In very hot conditions it may lift its abdomen towards the sun to reduce heat absorption and allow the wings to shade the head and thorax slightly. **Larval stages** Similar to other Gomphids, taking 3–5 years to emerge. **Status and distribution** Not in UK. Elsewhere in the area it is common and widespread in suitable habitats, especially in France. It is rarer in the north, but there are records as far north as central Sweden.

Onychogomphus uncatus*

May be found in the south of the area in France. It is closely related to *O. forcipatus*, distinguishable morphologically by the characters given above. It is more likely to be found in clear, fast-flowing rivers, but otherwise it is ecologically similar.

▲ *Ophiogomphus serpentinus* ♂

▼ *Onychogomphus forcipatus* ♂

Family Aeshnidae
The 'Aeshna' Family

A large family comprising the dragonflies generally known as the hawkers together with the emperor dragonflies. All are large species, with long abdomens and strong flight – the epitome of a dragonfly.

Genus *Brachytron*

Comprising one species in the area.

Brachytron pratense   The Hairy Hawker

Size Abdomen length: male 40–46 mm, female rather shorter. Wingspan: 72 mm. **Flight period** April to early July (early May to early July in UK). **Description** A small to medium-sized, robust hawker, with noticeably hairy head and thorax in both sexes. **Males** have a brown thorax, with green stripes; abdomen black with paired blue spots on each segment except number one, which has a single yellow spot. Wing-costa yellow, and pterostigma extremely long and narrow. **Females** are similar to the male, but thoracic stripes much reduced, wing bases suffused with yellow, and abdomen hairy, with yellow markings. **Similar species** Several *Aeshnas*, especially *A. juncea* are rather similar. The best single character for *Brachytron* is its early flight period, and a closer look will show the hairy body, long pterostigma, and single spot on segment one to separate it from *Aeshnas*. **Habitat** A species of neutral or occasionally acid lakes, canals, slow-moving rivers and ditches, yet absent from many apparently suitable sites. In the UK, particularly associated with floodplain or coastal levels with numerous ditches, e.g. in Somerset and Sussex. **Behaviour** The very early flight period is characteristic. Males remain close to water (unlike many *Aeshna spp.*) and fly low but strongly up and down a regular beat, settling more frequently than *Aeshnas*. In breezy or cool weather, they may seek out warm glades in woodland. Females are more inconspicuous, and only come to water to breed. The female lays eggs alone, into floating weed, rotting plant material or emergent plants. A distinctive species, readily recognised once learnt. **Larval stages** Weed-dwellers, usually taking several years to mature, though they may only take one year in favourable conditions. Length about 35–40 mm. **Status and distribution** A notable species in the UK, now virtually confined to southern England. It is declining as its habitats become drained or polluted, especially where damp rough grazing land gives way to fertilised leys or arable crops. In Europe, it is widespread right throughout the area, but never really common, and rare in the northern part. Possibly overlooked.

▲ *Brachytron pratense* ♂   ▼ *Brachytron pratense* ♀

Genus *Aeshna*

A genus comprising nine species in the area. They are a distinctive group, known collectively as the hawkers, distinguishable from most other groups by their large size and powerful tireless flight. The most similar other genera are *Anax*, *Brachytron* and *Cordulegaster*, but the main problems of identification lie within the genus. Apart from *A. grandis* and *A. isosceles*, the remainder have many similarities and may require close examination for certain identification. The following Key together with the photographs and descriptions should help to separate them. If in England, or equivalent latitude, it is most likely that any difficult species will be resolved by reference to the table under *Aeshna juncea* first.

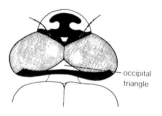

Fig. 39   Eyes and occipital triangle of *Aeshna caerulea*

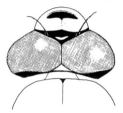

Fig. 40   Forehead and marking (incomplete T-shape) of *Aeshna viridis*

Fig. 41   *Aeshna juncea* thoracic markings

Fig. 42   *Aeshna subarctica* thoracic markings

Key to species of the genus *Aeshna*

1   Thorax and abdomen pale brown, without distinct markings except for a yellow triangle on segment two; eyes green, wings clear except at base; rare spring species   *A. isosceles* (page 104)

—   Not as above   **2**

2   Thorax and abdomen predominantly dark brown with very small patches of blue (in male) and yellow; wings strongly suffused brownish-orange; no segment two triangle. Common   *A. grandis* (page 100)

—   Abdomen strongly marked with blue, yellow or green   **3**

3   Distinct blue or yellow coloured triangle visible on segment two   **4**

—   No clearly-visible triangle on segment two   **6**

4   Segment two triangle elongated, yellow; colour on segments nine and ten unbroken, forming blue or greenish band over whole dorsal surface; broad thoracic stripes present   *A. cyanea* (page 98)

—   Colour on segments nine and ten broken by black to form two spots on each; thoracic stripes indistinct or absent   **5**

5   Triangle yellow in both sexes: thorax marked on sides with two large yellow patches between sutures strongly outlined in black   *A. mixta* (page 102)

—   Triangle blue in males, yellow in females; thorax laterally yellow with blue-green suffusion without large yellow patches; sutures finely outlined in black. Not in UK, southern only   *A. affinis** (page 104)

6   Eyes only contiguous for a very short distance, less than or equal to length of occipital triangle (see fig. 39). All markings bright blue (or dull blue in female). Mountains and northern areas only   *A. caerulea* (page 96)

—   Eyes contiguous for longer than length of occipital triangle. Markings blue, green or yellow   **7**

7   Wings lightly cloudy throughout; T-shaped black mark on forehead incomplete (see fig. 40). Sides of thorax green-striped; rare species, N. Germany and northwards only   *A. viridis** (page 96)

—   Wings mainly clear. T-shape on forehead complete   **8**

8   Thorax usually with broad yellow bands on side; without yellow mark below spiracle (see fig. 41); eyes bluish or brownish; two yellow spots present behind the head; a common species through all our area except for lowland France   *A. juncea* (page 94)

—   Thorax usually with broad blue or blue-green bands on side, yellowish markings below spiracle present (see fig. 42); eyes greenish; back of head black, without yellow spots (except in newly-emerged individuals); abdomen with *small* blue or yellow spots on segments 3–10, giving impression of a rather dark abdomen. Not in the UK   *A. subarctica** (page 98)

Aeshna juncea The Common Hawker

Size Abdomen length: 51–57 mm. Wingspan: 95 mm. **Flight period** Late June to September or even early October. **Description Males** are predominantly brown with thin yellow thoracic stripes, and blue markings on every abdominal segment. Wing costa (front margin) strongly coloured yellow. No distinct triangle on segment two. **Females** are similar, but shorter and thicker-bodied, with green markings in place of blue on the abdomen (usually), and thoracic stripes absent. **Similar species** Most other Aeshnas. *A. subarctica* is especially close (see Key, page 93) but very much rarer and more restricted. Over most of the area except the extreme south and north, the three species most likely to be confused are *A. juncea*, *A. cyanea*, and *A. mixta* and the following summarises their key points:

A. juncea: Bright yellow costa, no triangle on segment two, separate spots on segments nine and ten, thoracic stripes thin (absent in female).

A. cyanea: Costa brownish, large yellow triangle on segment two, unbroken bands on segments nine and ten, thoracic stripes very broad.

A. mixta: Costa brownish, small yellow triangle on segment two, separate spots on segments nine and ten, thoracic stripes absent or very indistinct.

In flight, *A. juncea* looks brown and blue, *A. cyanea* looks greener, and *A. mixta* looks smaller and darker, but this is a rough guide only. **Habitat** A very widespread species, primarily of acidic still-water areas, usually in upland or heathland regions. The size of the water body is unimportant, though most sites are well-vegetated and sheltered. Occasionally breeds in flushes in moorland areas. A strong-flying hawker, most often seen flying in and out of vegetation along pond and lake edges, but also frequently occurs in forest rides and lanes. Continues flying until dusk and later in warm weather. Individuals do not settle often, except in poor weather, or when mating (which is a long process, lasting several hours). Like most Aeshnas, it tends to settle in a 'hanging' position, rather than flat. Males are aggressive and territorial, though more individuals seem to fit into a given site than, for example *Anax*. They will often grab females that are still egg-laying after pairing, and attempt to pair with them again. Females lay, unpaired, into floating vegetation or damp moss. **Larval stages** A typical Aeshnid: the larva is large (about 45 mm long) and highly predatory. They live amongst aquatic plants or emergent vegetation. **Status and distribution** Common and widespread throughout (except in lowland France) though with a definite northern and upland preference, absent from the lowlands further south, though in lowland England it is common locally in heathy areas. Most abundant in the north of the area.

▲ *Aeshna juncea* ♂   ▼ *Aeshna juncea* ♀

Aeshna caerulea   The Azure Hawker or Blue Aeshna

Size Abdomen length: 42–48 mm. Wingspan: 80 mm. **Flight period** Early June to late August, or early September. **Description** A medium-sized hawker. **Males** are very blue in appearance with wholly blue markings on a dark brown base colour; two small blue thoracic stripes; eyes blue, face yellow. **Females** are duller with smaller, less bright blue markings; no thoracic stripes. **Similar species** Rather similar to all the 'coloured' *Aeshnas* and most likely to be confused with *A. juncea* as the habitats overlap. The wholly blue markings, the barely touching blue eyes and the square (rather than round) spots on segment nine of the female are characteristic. **Habitat** An upland species, associated particularly with shallow bog pools, with an active *Sphagnum* zone; usually sheltered and close to woodland. **Behaviour** Frequently settles on boulders and stones (unlike most *Aeshnas*) or occasionally on tree-trunks, but flies strongly when it takes off. On sunny days they are active in the morning, sometimes settling to avoid the hottest part of the day, often adopting a raised abdomen posture to keep cool. Adults may disperse widely from their larval habitat, into forests or along streams and are most often found in woodland clearings. Females lay unaccompanied into living *Sphagnum*, shallow water or emergent plants. **Larval stages** The larvae live at the bottom of pools, amongst debris, and take at least three years to mature. They are about 37– 38 mm long. **Status and distribution** In the UK this species is confined to Scotland with a mainly westerly distribution. It is widely spread there, but never common; absent from the remainder of the area except in southern Sweden and the Alps.

Aeshna viridis *

Size Abdomen length: 47–54 mm. Wingspan: 88 mm. **Flight period** Late July to early October. **Description** Generally similar to other *Aeshna* species except that both sexes have wings lightly suffused with brown. **Males** are basically brown with blue and green abdomen spots, broad green thoracic stripes and green eyes. **Females** are similar but more distinctly greenish, especially on the sides of thorax and abdomen, than other species. **Similar species** Most similar in general appearance to *A. cyanea* but the suffused wings, incomplete 'T' mark on the forehead (see Key and fig. 40), lack of yellow triangle, and interrupted colour bands on segments nine and ten are clear enough. Other *Aeshnas* are similar, and the key should be consulted if in doubt. **Habitat** Occurs in still fen-like ponds and lakes, usually well-vegetated, overlapping considerably with other species especially *A. grandis*. Particularly associated with the presence of water soldier *Stratiotes aloides*. **Behaviour** Most similar to *Aeshna grandis* species. The female lays eggs alone, into the leaves of *Stratiotes* for preference, but other aquatic plants are used. **Larval stages** Analogous with *A. grandis* in all respects. **Status and distribution** Not in the UK. In Europe, known only from the northern parts of the area, from N. Germany and Holland northwards. It is rare and declining. In more populous areas it has suffered from having its egg-laying plant, *Stratiotes*, removed by anglers since it is liable to take over ponds with its dominant growth.

▲ *Aeshna caerulea* ♂   ▼ *Aeshna viridis* ♂

Aeshna cyanea   The Southern Hawker

Size Abdomen length: 51–60 mm. Wingspan: 95–100 mm. **Flight period** End of June until early October. **Description** A large, predominantly greenish-looking species. **Males** possess a dark brown-black ground colour, strongly marked with broad green thoracic stripes and green spots on the abdomen except in segments 8–10 where they are blue, and on segment two where there is a bright yellow triangle. The colour on segments nine and ten (and almost on eight) is joined to form a band rather than spots. **Females** are very similar, but green not blue on segments 8–10. The costa is dull brown in both sexes. **Similar species** Similar to most of the other *Aeshnas*. See *A. viridis** for distinctions from that species, and under *A. juncea* for a comparison of *juncea*, *cyanea*, and *mixta*. **Habitat** Occurs in a broad variety of sites, especially in still acid waters of all sizes, but also in ditches, slow-moving streams, water tanks, and garden ponds. Will colonise gravel pits and other newly-created sites as they begin to vegetate. **Behaviour** A strong flier, well-known for its inquisitiveness, often flying up close to the observer (and possibly the cause of stories that dragonflies attack humans). One of the few dragonflies that will continue flying in dull, even damp, weather and on into the night. When individuals do settle, they may remain settled for long periods and are not too difficult to approach. They prefer to hang from a bush rather than settle on the ground or a tree. Individuals of either sex occur far from water, especially along lanes and forest rides, but also in towns. Mating always takes place high up in trees; the female then detaches and commences egg-laying into water plants, or – characteristically – damp inert material near water, such as logs, soil, or even concrete. **Larval stages** A weed-dweller, analogous with other species, though noted for frequently occuring at high densities in ponds, tanks or other small habitats. **Status and distribution** In the UK it is common and wide-spread throughout most of England, rarer in the north. It has been found recently at several Scottish sites and may be extending its range. In Europe it is common and widespread throughout the area, even in S. Scandinavia.

*Aeshna subarctica**

This species is extremely similar to *A. juncea*, distinguishable solely by the characters in the Key and minor differences in genitalia. It is also possible to distinguish the larvae or exuviae on a whole complex of characters and measurements, too detailed to include here. Reference should be made to Clausen (see Bibliography) if anyone wishes to attempt this.

A. subarctica is an uncommon species occurring in bogs and moorland pools especially with Schwingmoor from Germany and the Vosges north-eastwards only, with a requirement for living *Sphagnum*. The flight period is from July to September. It should be watched for in areas such as Scotland, since it is readily overlooked, through confusion with *A. juncea* , though any wholly new records would need a specimen for confirmation.

▲ *Aeshna cyanea* ♂   ▼ *Aeshna cyanea* ♀

Aeshna grandis The Brown Aeshna or The Brown Hawker

Size Abdomen length: males 54–60 mm; females 49–55 mm. Wingspan: 102 mm. **Flight period** Early June to October (early July to early October in UK). **Description** A very distinctive large and beautiful dark brown species with only small amounts of blue and yellow markings; wings strongly suffused with amber-brown, easily visible even in flight. **Male** has a 'waisted' appearance at segments 2–3, and blue spots on these segments. **Females** are very similar but abdomen is thicker throughout, without blue spots. **Similar species** Not readily confused with any other species: the dark brown body, and suffused wings are distinctive. *A. isosceles* may appear similar in pictures, but the flight periods rarely overlap, and the clear wings, paler body, yellow triangle and green eyes of *isosceles* are clear distinctions. **Habitat** Almost invariably found on medium to large lakes and ponds, which are usually well-vegetated and unpolluted. It prefers less acid waters than most other *Aeshnas*, and occurs in quite calcareous lakes. Suitable gravel pits are colonised, but only as they become vegetated and it is not an early coloniser. Occasionally occurs in slow-moving water, especially canals. **Behaviour** Broadly similar to other *Aeshnas*. A tireless flier, hawking in seemingly endless fashion along the edges of lakes, or often out over a patch of floating vegetation towards the middle. Males are strongly territorial but are unusual in that they may defend territory away from water. Less likely to be found in woods than other species, but it does move towards towns at times, and will often settle on walls in the evening sun. It tends to settle much more on vertical surfaces – trees, walls, etc – than on vegetation. They will chase almost any insect prey, up to and including large butterflies and other dragonflies. They will occasionally fly on after dusk and are even attracted to street lights. Pairing and laying is typical for the genus. **Larval stages** A large voracious weed-dweller, very strongly marked with yellow spots and striped legs. Length 45–50 mm. **Status and distribution** Common and widespread through most of England, though rare in the north and west, and absent from Scotland. Surprisingly absent from the south-west peninsula from Cornwall to West Somerset. In Europe, it is widespread and reasonably common, occurring in most suitable habitats but never abundantly.

▲ *Aeshna grandis* ♂   ▼ *Aeshna grandis* ♀

Aeshna mixta   The Migrant Hawker

Size Abdomen length: 44–50 mm. Wingspan: 85–88 mm. **Flight period** Early July to October (late July to October in UK). **Description** A smaller species than most of the genus, appearing rather darker in flight than *A. juncea* or *A. cyanea*. Both sexes have a dull brown costa, and lack dorsal thoracic stripes. **Males** are predominantly dark brown with the abdomen well-marked with blue spots, a cream-yellow patch on segment three, and a yellowish triangle on segment two. **Females** have a similar ground colour, but with duller greenish abdominal markings; anal appendages very long. **Similar species** Rather similar to most other *Aeshnas spp.* especially *A. juncea*. See *A. juncea* for comparative table. *A. mixta* does look smaller in flight (once you are familiar with the other species) and a tentative identification may often be made on the basis of its more sociable behaviour (see below). *A. affinis,** which just occurs in the south of the area, is very similar in most respects. The differences are described in the Key (see page 93), and under *A. affinis* below. **Habitat** Breeds in still-waters which may vary from rather acid to slightly calcareous. Brackish water is also tolerated, and it may occur, like most species, in slow-moving water such as canals; well-vegetated sites with marginal tall vegetation, or reedy ditches, seem to be preferred. It is, however, a highly migratory insect and individuals or groups may be found almost anywhere, including in towns and over the sea. **Behaviour** Distinctly different from most *Aeshnas* in that the males are non-territorial, and seem also to be sociable, such that it is quite common to see six or more sharing the same 'beat'. It hovers frequently and a whole group may remain in one position, but will also often fly up very high in pursuit of prey, and can fly very quickly when it chooses to. These characteristics will often allow an 'instant' identification to be made, to be confirmed by a closer view if possible. In other respects, it is similar to other *Aeshna* species. **Larval stages** Analogous with other *Aeshnas*. A weed-dweller sometimes occurring in brackish water. Smaller than average, with a length of about 35 mm. **Status and distribution** Once considered only as a migrant in the UK but now well-established and relatively common throughout lowland England. The resident populations are regularly reinforced by migrants. Absent from the north and west, but spreading slowly and able to make use of new habitats because of its wide travelling ability. In Europe, it is common and widespread, especially in the south, but occurring as far north as N. Germany and Denmark, and south Sweden.

▲ *Aeshna mixta* ♂

▼ *Aeshna mixta* ♀

Aeshna affinis*

This species is similar to *A. mixta*. It occurs rarely in the southern parts of the area or more commonly further south in Europe. It is analogous in most respects to *A. mixta* and readily confused with it, except for the morphological differences and the fact that *A. affinis* remains paired during egg-laying (unusually amongst *Aeshna* species). *A. affinis* appears to be much bluer than *A. mixta* but it is essential to look at the sides of the thorax for certain identification, as described in the Key (see page 93). The flight is weaker and *A. affinis* tends to 'hover' more.

Aeshna isosceles   The Norfolk Hawker

(Sometimes placed in the genus *Anaciaeschna* on the basis of differences in wing venation and coloration.) **Size** Abdomen length: 48–53 mm. Wingspan: 90–95 mm. **Flight period** Mid-May to end of July (late May to early July in UK). **Description** A distinctive species as much for its early flight period as its appearance. Males and females are extremely similar. The general colour is light brown throughout, broken only by the distinctive yellow triangle on segment two, the beautiful green eyes, and a dark stripe on segments eight and nine. **Similar species** Unlikely to be confused with any other species by virtue of its highly distinctive appearance and early flight period. See *A. grandis* (see page 100) for distinctions from that species. **Habitat:** In Britain, this species is highly restricted in habitat, occurring only in a few well-vegetated unpolluted ditches, though once it occurred more widely in the Norfolk Broads. In the rest of the area, it is a species of well-vegetated lakes, of about neutral pH, or ditches on levels. Further south, it occurs in a wider variety of habitats. **Behaviour** Broadly similar to other *Aeshna* species. Tends to remain closer to its larval habitat than most of the genus, and is most often seen over or by water. Settles more readily than most, usually on trees or bushes but also on walls. The female lays alone into floating vegetation or debris, or into submerged plants. **Larval stages** A weed-dweller, analogous with other species, and taking 2–3 years to mature. Length: 40–43 mm. **Status and distribution** In the UK this species is now severely restricted and endangered. Pollution of the Norfolk Broads, where it was more widespread, has left it confined to a few ditch systems where it is highly vulnerable to agricultural changes. Elsewhere within the area, it occurs throughout as far north as Denmark and south Sweden, though it is local everywhere and never abundant. It is essentially a mediterranean species, and only becomes common outside the area.

▲ *Aeshna affinis* ♂

▼ *Aeshna isosceles* ♂

Genus *Anax*

A small genus of two species in Europe, similar in general form and size to the *Aeshnas* but quite different in colour and markings. Both species have a continuous black line down the top of the abdomen.

Anax imperator   The Emperor Dragonfly

Size Abdomen length: males 53–61 mm; females 49–55 mm. Wingspan: 105–108 mm. In most respects, the largest dragonfly in the area. **Flight period** May to September, usually starting in the second half of May in the UK. **Description** A large, robust, species. **Males** The head, thorax and first segment of abdomen all mid-green; the abdomen is basically a bright turquoise-blue, with a black stripe running the whole length centrally. There is a distinct 'waist' at segment three. The wing-bases are more rounded than those of *Aeshna*. **Females** are similar in markings but the base-colour is green throughout, except for the tip of the abdomen which is brownish. There is no abdominal 'waist'. **Similar species** The colour and the black line dorsally on the abdomen distinguish this species easily in the UK. In parts of the area where *A. parthenope** occurs, this may be confused. *A. parthenope* males, however, have an abdomen that is dull greenish-brown from segment two or three onwards and the sides of the thorax are brown (not green) in both sexes. The abdomen is also slightly more slender. **Habitat** A still water species, occurring in ponds, lakes, gravel pits, canals and other similar habitats. Although preferring well-vegetated sheltered sites, it will also colonise quite newly-created situations, and may breed in brackish water. **Behaviour** *Anax* shows a greater preference for feeding over and around water than many *Aeshna* species and it is most often seen flying over the water or settled on the outer edges of marginal vegetation. In flight, its abdomen seems to droop in a slight curve in contrast to the straight abdomen of *Aeshna* species. Prey is often taken apart on the wing, but then eaten when settled high in a tree. The females lay their eggs alone, into floating and submerged vegetation. This species has probably been more studied than any other dragonfly, and much general knowledge of dragonflies has derived from its study. **Larval stages** A characteristic weed-dweller, moving to floating vegetation in large numbers as emergence time approaches. Highly predatory, and very large (over 50 mm). **Status and distribution** Common and widespread through all the southern part of the area, though absent from Scandinavia (except Denmark) and Scotland. Common in south and central England, but virtually absent north of the Midlands.

*Anax parthenope**

Is very close to *A. imperator* and analogous in most respects. It occurs in similar habitats with a very similar distribution except that it is absent from the UK. Its habits and behaviour are similar except that females often remain paired during egg-laying. It is distinguished from *A. imperator* in the field by the features of colour described under *A. imperator* (see page 106).

▲ *Anax imperator* ♂   ▼ *Anax imperator* ♀

Family Cordulegasteridae

Genus *Cordulegaster*

A small family represented in the area by only two species in the genus *Cordulegaster*. They are species of fast-moving water, both distinctive by virtue of their golden-ringed appearance, and their barely-touching green eyes.

Cordulegaster boltonii   The Golden-ringed Dragonfly

Size Abdomen length: males 54–61 mm; females 61–65 mm. Wingspan: 100–104 mm. **Flight period** End of May until late September. **Description** The sexes are similar in most respects. They have a distinctive combination of a basically black body with golden-yellow rings on all thoracic segments, and bold yellow thoracic stripes. The eyes are green and rather pear-shaped, touching only at the points and the occipital triangle is yellow. The male has a slight 'waist' at segment three, while the female has a strikingly long ovipositor, making her the longest-bodied species in the area. **Similar species** No other species should be confused with *Cordulegaster* on careful examination. *C. bidentatus** is extremely similar but differs in having a black occipital triangle (not yellow), a wholly black ovipositor (not yellow at the base as in *C. boltonii*), and rather paler, smaller abdominal markings. **Habitat** Almost always occurs in and around flowing water, particularly well-oxygenated, fast-flowing acidic streams and rivers. It also occurs very occasionally in ponds or lakes. The most frequent larval habitat is in calmer stretches or pools in fast rivers with sandy or gravelly bottoms, but the adults will wander widely from this situation, and can be encountered on moorland or heathland far from any water. **Behaviour** Notable for its strong direct purposeful flight, from which it is much less likely to be deflected than an *Aeshna*. The males, especially, hawk up and down streams or along the edges of water, or in a wider circuit including drier habitats. Females will fly slowly but strongly up streams – on overgrown stretches they can be heard thrusting through the vegetation – ovipositing in suitable sites. The manner of egg-laying is impressive to watch, as she stabs her ovipositor deeply and strongly into the gravel, from a vertical position, firmly implanting the eggs into the substrate. Both sexes will settle on boulders or vegetation – where they hang like an *Aeshna* – and are then not difficult to approach. **Larval stages** The larvae of *C. boltonii* spend most of their life buried in mud with their head and front legs exposed, and usually the tip of the abdomen, to allow respiration to take place. They take at least three to four years to mature, longer in upland streams. **Status and distribution** In Britain, this is a northern and western species, following the distribution of its preferred habitat, though it is absent from Ireland. It is most frequent in S.W. England and W. Scotland, though never abundant. It is widespread throughout the area in Europe, though rare in lowland agricultural areas, and never very common.

Cordulegaster bidentatus

Is very similar to *C. boltonii* in all respects, though it is rarer and slightly more exacting in habitat, preferring colder more oxygenated waters and smaller streams. It can be separated by the characters given under *C. boltonii* (above).

▲ *Cordulegaster boltonii* ♂   ▼ *Cordulegaster boltonii* ♀

Family Corduliidae   The Emerald Dragonflies

A family of four genera and six species in N. Europe. All the species, except *Epitheca* are 'emeralds' and have distinctive green, often metallic, bodies.

Genus *Cordulia*

Cordulia aenea   The Downy Emerald

Size Abdomen length: 34–38 mm. Wingspan: 70 mm. **Flight period** Mid-May to early August. **Description** Both sexes similar. They have a bronze-green, downy thorax, a dark metallic green abdomen, and green eyes. The wings are clear except for amber patches at their bases, though those of older females become bronzed or yellowed. Females have rounded wing-bases, whilst males have more angular bases, and the male has a distinct waist and corresponding club tail, which the female lacks. **Similar species** *Somatochlora metallica* and *S. arctica* (See pages 112–113) are particularly similar, and the former may frequently occur with *Cordulia*. In flight, the *Somatochlora metallica* looks distinctly more metallic (unless they are old specimens), though a closer view is usually required. Both *Somatochlora spp.* have yellow on the sides of their faces (see fig. 43) sometimes visible in flight; male *Somatochlora spp.* have much longer anal appendages and usually have amber-coloured wings. *Cordulia* appears several weeks earlier. **Habitat** Mainly still waters, of all kinds. It has a slight preference for acidic lakes but also occurs in neutral and even calcareous sites. Sheltered well-wooded sites are usually preferred, and the adults are often found in woodland clearings. **Behaviour** Males, in particular, fly low along the margins of ponds, back and forth along a regular beat which follows each inlet. They will often hover in a favoured spot, but settle only rarely except in poor weather. Both sexes disperse into woodland, and females particularly seem to feed in sheltered glades. The female lays alone, by striking the surface of the water hard, each time depositing a mass of eggs. **Larval stages** The small long-legged larvae live amongst debris and weeds, and may carry a cover of debris around with them. Length 20–25 mm. **Status and distribution** In the UK this is a notable species virtually confined to south central England but with a very few sites elsewhere, including in Cumbria and north Scotland (where it was recently rediscovered). In the rest of the area, it is widespread and frequent (though rarely abundant) throughout. The reason for this species' distribution in Britain is a mystery.

Genus *Epitheca*

*Epitheca bimaculata**

Size Abdomen length: 39–42 mm. Wingspan: 84 mm. **Flight period** May to July. **Description** Males and females are similar. The overall colour impression is brown; the thorax is dull brown or greenish-brown, with numerous short hairs; the abdomen has a broad central blackish stripe, and the sides are orange-brown, clearly visible in flight or at rest. There is a conspicuous dark patch at the base of the hindwings, and the wings themselves become cloudy.

*Cordulia
aenea* ♂

*Epitheca
bimaculata*
♂

Similar species Quite different from other emeralds in superficial appearance and more likely to be confused with *Libellula quadrimaculata* (see page 120). The latter always has a dark spot halfway along the front margin of the wing and often another at the end, and it is a squatter species with a shorter abdomen. **Habitat** Still waters, particularly larger areas, including lakes and ponds and occasionally marshy areas with ditches. The adults can also be found well away from their larval habitats. **Behaviour** Distinctive in the method of egg-laying. After mating, the female perches on vegetation, and extrudes a 'lump' of eggs in a gelatinous mass. She then flies to an egg-laying site and trails her abdomen in the water, allowing the mass to unroll into a string of hundreds, or even thousands, of eggs. The flight is faster than other emeralds with less tendency to 'patrol' edges of lakes. **Larval stages** Usually weed-dwellers, taking 2–3 years to mature. **Status and distribution** An eastern species, absent from the UK and most of France and rare elsewhere.

Genus *Oxygastra**

Oxygastra curtisii   The Orange-spotted Emerald

Size Abdomen length: 36–39 mm. Wingspan: 72 mm. **Flight period** June to August. **Description** Very similar to other 'emeralds' in shape and size, but particularly distinctive in that both sexes have a band of orange spots down the back of the abdomen, and these are clearly visible on both sexes and in newly-emerged specimens. The sexes are very similar, except that the female has wings which are suffused with amber and have rounded bases, while the male has clear wings with angular bases. The eyes are green. **Similar species** Although similar to *Somatochlora* and *Cordulia* (the other emeralds) it is readily distinguished by the orange-spotted abdomen when settled. **Habitat** In the UK, this was a species of small–medium rivers, intermediate in character between sluggish lowland rivers and well-oxygenated fast-flowing rivers. Elsewhere it is mainly a river species, but also occurs in canals and even lakes and fish ponds occasionally. They do not wander far from the larval habitat. **Behaviour** Not particularly distinctive. The males are territorial and have a 'beat' which they fly around, though if disturbed they will fly off rapidly, often to a great height. They have a rather weaker flight than *Cordulia*, and tend to settle more readily. Otherwise, very similar to the other emeralds in general behaviour. **Larval stages** Mud-dwellers, often partially buried in the mud. They take 2–3 years to develop and are rarely found. Length 22–24 mm. **Status and distribution** In Britain, this species has never been recorded more than a few times, and has not been seen for many years. Its final extinction is presumed to have been caused by the construction of a sewage treatment plant near its known site (that had effluent *within* the permitted levels of quality set by the water authority), though this species was clearly right on the edge of its range in Britain. Elsewhere, it is only really likely to be found in France (it is primarily an Iberian species) though there are occasional records for Holland, Germany and Belgium. It is a rare and important species anywhere within the area.

Genus *Somatochlora*

Somatochlora metallica   The Brilliant Emerald

Size Abdomen length: 37–40 mm. Wingspan: 75–80 mm. **Flight period** Mid-June to early September. **Description** Males and females similar. Both have a brilliant metallic green or bronze-green thorax and abdomen, with green eyes. The sides of the thorax are covered with yellowish down. The wings are suffused with amber, more so in the females. Males have a distinct 'waist' at segments 3–4, and more angular wing bases. **Similar species** Extremely similar to *S. arctica*, and only certainly separable on close examination. *S. arctica* is slightly darker and less metallic-looking, has an *isolated* yellow spot on each side of the face; see fig. 43 (joined by a yellow bar in *S. metallica*), and the male has distinctly curved 'pincer-like' appendages; see fig. 44 (straighter in *S. metallica*). The female *metallica* has a very pronounced sharp vulvar scale under segments 9–10 (see fig. 45). See also *Cordulia aenea* and *S. flavomaculata*. **Habitat** Very similar to *Cordulia*, i.e. neutral to acid still waters and canals. There is a strong preference for sites with some over-

continued on page 114

Oxygastra
curtisii
♀

Somatochlora
metallica
♂

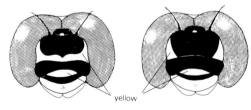

Somatochlora metallica   *Somatochlora arctica*

Fig. 43   Faces of *Somatochlora spp.*

hanging vegetation – under which the female lays – but not overshaded sites. **Behaviour** Very similar to *Cordulia* in most respects. During egg-laying, the tip of the abdomen is bent upwards, and then the whole abdomen is forcefully struck downwards into the mud or through the surface of shallow water. In some sites, the eggs are laid into *sphagnum* around the margins of ponds. **Larval stages** Similar ecologically to *Cordulia* (see page 110). **Status and distribution** In the UK, this has a curious disjunct distribution with numerous sites in central southern England, a few sites in N. Scotland, and nowhere else. This is particularly strange, since in Europe it is widespread and frequent, though only abundant, in Scandinavia.

Somatochlora arctica The Northern Emerald

Size Abdomen length: 37–40 mm. Wingspan: 68–70 mm. **Flight period** Mid-May to September (late May to August in UK). **Description** Very similar to *S. metallica* (see page 112), though rather darker; the male anal appendages are caliper-like (see fig. 44), and the vulvar scale is short and blunt (see fig. 45), while segment three of the female's abdomen has an orange spot on each side and the face has an isolated yellow spot on either side in both sexes (see fig. 43). **Similar species** See particularly *S. metallica* and *S. flavomaculata*, both of which occur with it in places. **Habitat** Peaty pools frequently with *Sphagnum* moss, and most commonly near woodland or scattered trees. Especially favours clearings in pine forests large enough to sustain sunny pools. Always either northern or montane. **Behaviour** Similar to *S. metallica* but with less tendency to 'patrol' pond edges. The female lays alone, usually into *Sphagnum* or wet peat and mud, flicking the eggs in with her abdomen bent. **Larval stages** A burrower in dense *Sphagnum* debris. No ventral or dorsal spines. Little is known of its feeding habits in the wild. **Status and distribution** In the British Isles, occurs in N. Scotland and Kerry only, where it is local but not uncommon. In Europe it is absent from the lowlands in the south of the area, but not uncommon in hilly areas up to around 2000 m, and widespread throughout northern areas.

*Somatochlora flavomaculata**

Size Abdomen length: 34–40 mm. Wingspan: 75 mm. **Flight period** Mid-May to end of August. **Description** Very similar in general shape and colour to other *Somatochlora spp.*, but it has distinctive yellow stripes on the side of the thorax, and yellow markings *laterally* on all segments of the abdomen, especially visible on two and three. The female vulvar scale is erect but short. **Similar species** Other *Somatochloras* are similar but lack the yellow markings. *Epitheca bimaculata* (see page 110) should also be looked at. **Habitat** The larval habitat is similar to *S. metallica*, though the adults are most often seen away from water, in woodland clearings, fields or lanes. **Behaviour** Very similar to *S. metallica*, though less likely to be seen hawking over water and unusual in that territories may be defended away from water. The males are rather less aggressive, and more easily approached. **Larval stages** Mud-dwellers, similar in appearance to those of *S. metallica*. **Status and distribution** Not in UK. Elsewhere, it is widespread throughout the area except in N.W. France. It is frequent though rarely abundant.

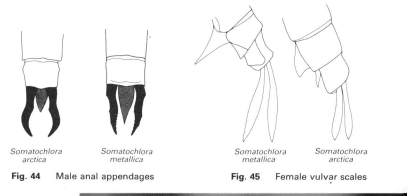

| Somatochlora arctica | Somatochlora metallica | Somatochlora metallica | Somatochlora arctica |

Fig. 44 Male anal appendages

Fig. 45 Female vulvar scales

Somatochlora
arctica
♀

Somatochlora
flavomaculata
♂

Family Libellulidae   The Chasers, Skimmers and Darters

An enormous family worldwide, represented in N. Europe by 23 species from five genera. Most are reasonably easy to identify to species level (given mature individuals) except for the darters *Sympetrum spp.* for which a separate Key is provided.

Genus *Libellula*

Comprises three species in the area, all of which have broad flattened abdomens and conspicuous dark brown patches at the base of the hindwings.

Libellula depressa   The Broad-bodied Chaser

Size Abdomen length: 24–28 mm. Wingspan: 76 mm. **Flight period** Mid-May to August in UK, or from late April further south. **Description** A squat, very broad-bodied species. **Males** have a mid-brown thorax with two broad yellowish stripes; in mature males, the whole abdomen is blue due to pruinescence, though the orange-brown sides are visible for much of its life. Both pairs of wings have dark brown patches at the bases, larger in the hindwings. **Females** and young males are similar except that the abdomen is brown or yellowish throughout, with more yellow at the sides. They may sometimes appear even broader than the males. **Similar species** The combination of broad body and dark wing patches distinguishes it from most species. The blue *Orthetrums* have clear wings and are more slender. *L. fulva* is more slender and has a diamond-shaped black tip over segments seven to ten in both sexes. *L. quadrimaculata* is never blue, and has an additional dark patch at the nodus of both wings. **Habitat** Occurs in a very wide variety of still or slow-flowing waters. Most common on small, sheltered, ponds with good marginal vegetation, and it is frequent on garden, or unpolluted farm, ponds. Also occurs in bog pools, if not too acid, but prefers neutral waters. Will colonise new habitats such as old gravel pits quite readily. It may breed in brackish water. Also wanders and migrates, so can be found almost anywhere. **Behaviour** An aggressive and strongly territorial species. Males will often take over a small pond, defending it against all intruders, and using the same perches day after day. Females spend more time away from water. Pairing takes place in the air: the male seizes the female, and the whole process is over in less than a minute, after which the female seeks out a laying site alone. **Larval stages** The larva lives either amongst aquatic plants or on the bottom mud and debris, but not habitually buried. It is about 26 mm long. **Status and distribution** In the UK, it is common and widespread over most of England and Wales, and has recently been found in Cumbria. It has suffered from the loss or pollution of farm ponds, but gained, to some extent, from new industrial habitats. It is absent from Ireland, but elsewhere it is common and widespread throughout except in the mountains.

▲ *Libellula depressa* ♂

▼ *Libellula depressa* ♀

Libellula fulva   The Scarce Chaser

Size Abdomen length: 26–29 mm. Wingspan: 75 mm. **Flight period** Early May to mid-August (late May to July in UK). **Description** A more slender species than *L. depressa*. **Males** The thorax is dark brown, unstriped and rather hairy; the abdomen is bright powder blue except for segments one to two which are darker, and a diamond-shaped tapering black patch from segment seven onwards. On all but newly-matured specimens, there are dark irregular patches on segments five to six, caused by mating – the spines of the female's legs remove the blue pruinescence at this point. The wings are clear except for the triangular brown patch at the base of the hindwings, though there may be a wingtip brown patch in some individuals. **Females** and young males are similar; the thorax is pale, and the abdomen is orange-brown with increasing black markings from segment three or four onwards. The wing tips usually have a brown patch as well as the basal patch in the females. **Similar species** Males may be confused with *Orthetrum cancellatum* (see page 120 for distinctions) also *L. depressa*. **Habitat** In Britain this is a rare species occurring in a few slow-moving rivers, some lakes and, recently, gravel pits. It prefers waters of approximately neutral pH status. Elsewhere, it is rather more widespread in most still water habitats, except very acid ones, and in rivers and canals. Sheltered sites are preferred. **Behaviour** Broadly similar to other *Libellula* species: notable for its mass synchronised emergence. Males are very active and territorial, yet they settle frequently (albeit rarely for long as any movement disturbs them). They settle more on logs and stones than *L. depressa*. Mating begins in the air, but unlike *L. depressa*, the pair usually settle, often for some while, to complete the process. The female then proceeds to lay into surface vegetation, without the male. Females spend much time perched on reeds or other vegetation, often a little way from the water. **Larval stages** A very spiny mud-dweller, about 25 mm long. The larva takes two or more years to mature. **Status and distribution** In the UK this is a rare species that has declined in recent decades. It is virtually restricted to central southern England and East Anglia, though it has begun to colonise some gravel pits and has recently been discovered in new sites. In continental Europe, however, it is widespread and locally common – in some areas, it occurs on almost every lake and canal, sometimes in large numbers.

Paired *Libellula fulva*

▲ *Libellula fulva* ♂

▼ Teneral (young) *Libellula fulva* ♂

Libellula quadrimaculata   The Four-spotted Chaser

Size Abdomen length: 27–32 mm. Wingspan: 72–80 mm. **Flight period** May to mid-August. **Description** Males and females very similar. Overall brown, but with very bright markings in mature but not aged specimens. The thorax is dark brown, with black on segment one and a black tip from segment seven to eight onwards. The sides of the thorax are yellow-orange, visible from above. The wings are distinctive with, in addition to the typical *Libellula* basal patches, a very distinct dark spot on each wing at the middle of the leading edge, and the pterostigma is dark and long. One form *praenubila*, has larger regular patches and additional wingtip patches. No blue colouring appears on the body at all. **Similar species** Not readily confused, particularly because of the wing markings. See females of other *Libellula spp.*, and also *Epitheca* (page 110) for distinctions from that species. **Habitat** A still water species. In Britain, it is most frequent in bog pools associated with heathland, but it also occurs in lakes, ponds, and brackish waters. Most abundant in acidic sites, especially if well-vegetated and shallow. In Europe, its requirements are similar, though it is more frequent on large lakes, and seems less affected by the pH of the water. It wanders considerably, and may be found well away from water. **Behaviour** A very active, aggressively territorial species, always interesting to watch. Males take up perches in the morning and vigorously defend an area against other males whilst looking for females. Territorial activity tends to die away in the afternoons. Mating takes place very rapidly in the air and in most respects it is very similar to *L. depressa*. **Larval stages** A mud-dweller, taking two to four years to mature. It is about 27 mm long. **Status and distribution** In the UK, this species is common and widespread throughout most of the country, though rather rarer in the east where suitable habitats are less frequent. In favoured sites, especially on heathland areas, it may be very abundant. Elsewhere in Europe it is very common and widespread throughout, and is found from the Mediterranean to beyond the Arctic Circle.

Genus *Orthetrum*

*Orthetrum albistylum**

Size Abdomen length: 32–24 mm. Wingspan: 75–80 mm. **Flight period** June to September. **Description** Both sexes are very similar to those of *O. cancellatum*. **Males** differ in having a more distinct truncated black-tipped narrower abdomen, as if dipped in black ink, on segments 7–10; distinctly white anal appendages, visible even in flight; a browner costa; and a generally neater, more dapper appearance readily noticeable even at a distance. **Females** are very similar to *O. cancellatum*, but the white anal appendages are diagnostic. **Similar species** Most similar to *O. cancellatum* but readily separated as described above and under that species. *Libellula fulva* might be confused, but the brown wing-patches, broader abdomen, lack of white anal appendages and diamond-shaped tapering black tip to abdomen are distinct in *fulva*. **Habitat** Stagnant and slow-flowing waters, especially well-vegetated lakes, ponds and canals. **Behaviour** Very similar to *O. cancellatum* with which it often occurs. **Larval stages** Analogous to those of *O. cancellatum*. **Status and distribution** Not in UK. Only occurs in central France and southern Germany where it is locally common. Further south, out of the area, it becomes frequent.

▲ *Libellula quadrimaculata* ♂   ▼ *Orthetrum albistylum* ♂

Orthetrum cancellatum   Black-tailed Skimmer

Size Abdomen length: 30–35 mm. Wingspan: 75–80 mm. **Flight period** Late April to September (late May to August in UK). **Description** The **male,** when seen in flight, gives the impression of a medium-sized blue and brown dragonfly. The abdomen is blue except for the tip (segments 8–10) which is black with the black suffusing up into the seventh segment. The sides of the abdomen are usually lined with orange, although in older individuals this may be obscured by blue. The thorax is brown, with two narrow black lines on top, which are not always clear. Both males and females have clear wings with a yellowish costal vein and black pterostigma. The **female** is dull yellow-brown with strong broad black curved markings on each abdominal segment. **Similar species** *O. albistylum** has almost the same overall coloration but is slenderer and smarter-looking, with a more clearly defined black-tipped abdomen. It has white abdominal appendages which are visible in flight, and no yellow costal vein. *Libellula fulva* (see page 118) has dark smokey triangles at the base of the hindwings – and to a lesser extent the forewings – and a more distinctive black diamond-shaped tip to the abdomen. The females, and occasionally the males, have smokey-brown wing-tips, which the Blacktailed Skimmer never has. See also *L. depressa* (page 116) and *Leucorrhinia caudalis* (page 142). **Habitat** In Britain, this is primarily a species of open still water, especially where the water has a hard bed such as occurs in farm ponds, dew ponds and a variety of similar situations. It also readily colonises flooded mineral workings if suitable. The acidity of the water is not critical, and it may occur in bogs and brackish conditions. Mature adults travel considerable distances, which allows them to colonise new habitats. Elsewhere in Europe, its habitats are similar to Britain although it also occurs along large rivers, e.g. the Loire in France. **Behaviour** As other *Orthetrum* species, although the males are noticeably more aggressive and powerful than those of *O. coerulescens* with more inclination to be territorial. Mating is a conspicuous affair, with the pairs flying noisily about for some time before settling for 15–20 minutes on the ground or in a bush to mate, rising in tandem if disturbed. They separate after mating and the female flies low over a suitable area of water, beating the water's surface with the tip of her abdomen each time she lays an egg. She may be led to water by the male. The males settle on vegetation or on the ground especially where it is bare. At rest the wings are held horizontally, not normally downwards as they are in *O. coerulescens*. **Larval stages** A mud-dweller, living on the bottom of pools amongst debris or silt. 28–30 mm long. **Status and distribution** In Britain, it is commonest in the Home Counties and Wessex, although scattered colonies occur over most of southern England. It may be very abundant where it is found, and has benefited from the production of suitable new breeding habitats created from the extensive gravel and sand workings around many south-eastern river valleys. Widespread and frequently abundant in the rest of N. Europe as far as S. Sweden, although it becomes progressively less common further north.

▲ *Orthetrum cancellatum* ♂

▼ *Orthetrum cancellatum* ♀

Orthetrum coerulescens   The Keeled Skimmer

Size Abdomen length: 27–30 mm. Wingspan: 60 mm. **Flight period** Early June to September in the UK; further south they appear in May. **Description   Males** The abdomen is wholly blue, bright but not metallic, and slenderer than comparable *Libellula* species. The thorax is dark brown, with two distinctive creamy-yellow stripes on top, though these may be duller in some individuals. The wings are clear, except for a faint amber smudge at the base of the hind pair, and the pale orange pterostigmas. In flight, especially, the wings appear very long in relation to the body. The **females** and young males are similar to each other in colour. Their pattern is broadly similar to that of the mature males, but the colouring is almost wholly yellow-brown, though the thoracic stripes still show as slightly paler and there are dark lines along each side of the abdomen. The wings are lightly suffused with orange-brown. The abdomen is narrower than that of the male. Females become bluish as they age. **Similar species** The most similar species in our area is *O. brunneum** which is rather larger than *O. coerulescens*, and has a distinctive blue thorax without cream stripes, bright blue eyes, and a shorter pterostigma (less than 3 mm long). The other two *Orthetrums* have black-tipped abdomens, and *Libellulla depressa* (page 116) is broader and squatter, with dark wing bases. **Habitat** In Britain, this is primarily a bog-species closely associated with *Sphagnum* and wet heath areas, as long as there is some open water, even a ditch. It does not usually wander far from the larval habitat. In southernmost England it becomes slightly less fussy, and in the southern part of Northern Europe it is very widespread in streams, lakes and ponds of varying acidity, as well as bogs, though rarely in fast-flowing waters. **Behaviour** The males fly rapidly, and unpredictably, keeping low over the ground or water, usually preferring to fly along edges, where, for example, water and land meet. They settle quite frequently, both on the ground and on vegetation. Although wary, they are not too difficult to approach, especially late in the season. They tend to fly up readily to investigate 'intruding' insects but are not particularly territorial and several may settle close together at times. Typically, the wings are held forwards and downwards when at rest. Females are much less active, spending most time, if not pairing or egg-laying, settled amongst vegetation often a little way from water. **Larval stages** Variable, according to habitat. They live amongst weeds, in *Sphagnum* or on mud and debris, and are quite mobile. They develop in about two years. Length about 20 mm. **Status and distribution** In the UK, this is a local species, most frequent in south and west England and Wales. In favoured areas with adequate suitable habitat, e.g. the New Forest, it may be very abundant at times. It is absent from virtually all of north and east Britain. Elsewhere in Europe, it is frequent and widespread right throughout the area even in mountain areas.

*Orthetrum
coerulescens*
♂

Paired
*Orthetrum
coerulescens*

*Orthetrum
coerulescens*
♀

*Orthetrum brunneum**

Size Abdomen length: 29–31 mm. Wingspan: 65 mm. **Flight period** June to September. **Description   Males** The body and eyes are entirely bright blue (but not metallic) when mature. The wings are clear, with a short brown ptero-stigma. It is a bulkier insect than *O. coerulescens*, closer to *cancellatum* in size. The **females** are very similar to *O. coerulescens* except for the larger size, shorter browner pterostigmas, and minor differences in genitalia structure. **Similar species** Males are distinctive as the only wholly blue species, but see *O. coerulescens* and *Libellula depressa* (page 116). **Habitat** Occurs in a wide range of open waters, especially lakes, canals, and larger ditches, but also in slow-moving rivers. Needs some bare ground adjacent to the site. **Behaviour** Analagous with *O. coerulescens* though more likely to be found on bare ground, rather than low vegetation, compared to that species. **Larval stages** The larvae live in mud in shallow water, usually still but occasionally slow-flowing. Very similar to *O. coerulescens*. **Status and distribution** Not in UK. A southern species, absent from N. Germany northwards, but increasingly fre-quent southwards, becoming quite common in the extreme south of the area.

Genus *Crocothemis*

*Crocothemis erythraea**

Size Abdomen length: 22–29 mm. Wingspan: 60 mm. **Flight period** May to October. **Description** When mature the **males** are a striking 'nail-varnish' red colour throughout the head, thorax and abdomen, with red eyes. The wings have conspicuous yellow patches at their bases, especially on the hindwings, and some red veins. The pterostigmas are long pale brown with very broad black nerves on the top and bottom. The abdomen is broad and flat compared to *Sympetrum* species, and the legs are red-brown. **Females** are very similar in shape but are a dull yellowish-brown throughout, with rather darker markings down the centre and sides of the abdomen. The legs are pale brown, wings similar to those of the male. Young males are coloured as females, but have longer anal appendages. **Similar species** The bright scarlet red colour (males) and the rather broad abdomen separate this from any similar *Sympetrums* (see pages 128–139) which all have a narrower, more or less 'waisted' abdomen. The pterostigma of *Crocothemis* is longer with very black nerves on either side. **Habitat** Primarily a still water species in lakes, fish ponds, etc. usually of about neutral pH. Occasionally in canals or calmer stretches of rivers. Further south, it occurs in brackish habitats. It is a highly mobile species and occurs far from its larval habitats. **Behaviour** The males are territorial, but not quite as vigorous as *Libellula* species. They settle readily on vegetation or the ground, but are rarely still for long, chasing up to investigate males, females or potential prey. They are sun-lovers, most active in very hot weather. Pairing normally takes place in the air, very rapidly similar to *Libellula* species (see page 116), but may take place on a perch in windy weather. The female then lays alone, sometimes guarded by the male. **Larval stages** Variable, mud or weed-dwellers according to the site. May occur at high densities. Length about 30 mm. **Status and distribution** Not in UK, though recorded in Jersey (Channel Islands). In Mediterranean Europe, it is very abundant in favourable years and may migrate far into Northern Europe if conditions are right (e.g. in 1976). It breeds within the area regularly in north and central France, and in south Germany.

Orthetrum brunneum ♂

Crocothemis erythraea ♂

Crocothemis erythraea ♀

Genus *Sympetrum*   The Darters

A genus with ten species in our area, of which nine have males with reddish abdomens. They are very similar in general characteristics, and may be extremely difficult to differentiate with certainty in the field. Males are easier to separate than females. The following Key and descriptions endeavour to rely on field characters (some of which need close examination or very clear photographs) though the primary distinctions may only be seen with the aid of a microscope. Some doubt has been cast on *S. nigrescens* as a species in view of the number of intermediates between it and *S. striolatum* and lack of accuracy in the original description, but it is included here until the matter is resolved.

Key to species of the genus *Sympetrum* *(males only)*

Those marked * do not occur in the UK; those marked ** are rare vagrants or migrants in the UK.

1 All four wings have a prominent irregular brownish patch across the whole wing near the pterostigma. Rare   *S. pedemontanum** (page 138)

— Wings lacking brownish patches in this position, though many may have orange patches on wing bases   **2**

2 Legs (femurs and tibias) entirely black   **3**

— Legs black and yellow in stripes, or all yellow. Never all black   **4**

— Legs virtually all yellow with barely any black   *S. meridionale** (page 132)

3 Abdomen in both sexes brownish-black; thorax with black triangle in centre (or all black), sides black with yellow stripes. Pterostigma black. No red on body   *S. danae* (page 130)

— Abdomen red in mature males; no black triangle on thorax, which is reddish or yellowish, abdomen distinctly 'waisted'   *S. sanguineum* (page 132) (including *S. depressiusculum** – see page 132)

4 Wings with at least the basal quarter strongly marked with amber, usually more, and distinctly more in females   *S. flaveolum** (page 134)

— Wings with less than a quarter coloured amber   **5**

5 Wings with many veins red, pterostigma yellowish with strong black edges; face with large black patch on forehead; first abdominal segment black; second with black triangular mark, and red visible between the two   *S. fonscolombii** (page 134)

— Wings with veins black or yellow to red-brown; other characters not all as above   *S. striolatum group* (opposite)

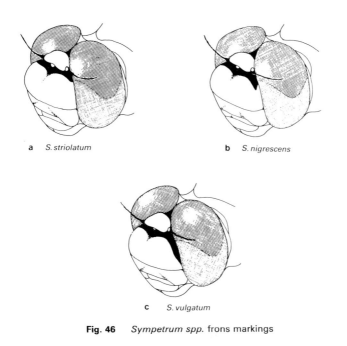

a   *S. striolatum*   b   *S. nigrescens*

c   *S. vulgatum*

Fig. 46   *Sympetrum spp.* frons markings

In N. Europe, the *striolatum* group comprises three very similar species, separable only on minor details. They may be distinguished, with care, as follows:

— Narrow black band across frons not continuing down the sides of the eyes (see fig. 46a); sutures on thorax not strongly outlined in black; common throughout   *S. striolatum* (page 136)

— Narrow black band across frons continuing a short way down sides of eyes (see fig. 46b); sutures on thorax strongly outlined in black, with bright yellow between them. Abdomen with strong black marks in side (see photograph, page 139); N. Britain, Ireland and Norway only *S. nigrescens* (page 138)

— Black band across frons continuing well down sides of eyes (see fig. 46c and photograph, page 137). Thorax and abdomen not as *nigrescens*, but abdominal segment one all black. Rare vagrant to UK, but common elsewhere in our area   *S. vulgatum*** (page 136)

Sympetrum danae (syn. *S. scoticum*)   The Black Darter

Size Abdomen length: 20–24 mm. Wingspan: 45–50 mm. **Flight period** Late June to October. **Description** Rather variable in colour according, mainly, to age. Mature **males** have thorax and abdomen all black, though younger males have yellow bands on the thorax and yellow down the centre of the abdomen. Legs black; wings clear with black pterostigma. Abdomen with distinct 'waist' at segments 3–5. **Females** are mainly yellow-brown with a distinctive black triangle on top of the thorax. Sides of the abdomen are marked with black. Wings with yellowed bases and black pterostigmas. **Similar species** May be confused with several other species according to the colour form. Fully-coloured males might be confused with *Cordulia aenea* (see page 110) which is much more greenish and the males (of *Cordulia*) have angular wing bases; teneral males might be mistaken for *Leucorrhinia dubia* (see page 140), but the wing-markings and thoracic stripes of *dubia* are distinctive and it is seen much earlier in the year. Only *S. sanguineum* and *S. depressiusculum** amongst *Sympetrums* have black legs, and these lack the dark thoracic triangle, and are usually red, or paler. **Habitat** Most frequently associated with acidic boggy waters; these may be bog pools, flushes or ditches of varying size and depth, but usually (though not necessarily) with active *Sphagnum* growth. Sheltered sites, e.g. in sunny woodland clearings, produce the highest densities. Also occurs in a few larger lakes, usually in acidic or upland areas. Individuals may be encountered well away from their larval habitats. **Behaviour** Typically, the males are not strongly territorial, and very large numbers of males, females and mixed tenerals will often occur together. Individuals can be more closely approached than most species, and, when they take flight, they soon settle again on vegetation or on the ground. They hunt mainly over ground or the water's edge. Pairing takes place in a settled position, and the female then lays either alone or still paired. **Larval stages** Variable, living amongst mud, peat, *Sphagnum* or aquatic vegetation, though usually in shallow water. Larval development can take place within one year in good conditions. Length about 17 mm. **Status and distribution** Primarily an upland or boreal species. In the UK, it is frequent in the north and west, and locally common in the south and east, wherever bogs or heathlands still exist. It occurs throughout Northern Europe, varying from local in the southern lowlands to extremely abundant in the north, often reaching very large numbers.

▲ *Sympetrum danae* ♂

▼ *Sympetrum danae* ♀

Sympetrum sanguineum   The Ruddy Darter

Size Abdomen length: 20–26 mm. Wingspan: 55 mm. **Flight period** June to October. **Description   Males** Thorax red-brown; abdomen blood-red, with black markings on segment one, down the centre of segments eight and nine, and along the sides from 4–8; there is a marked constriction of the abdomen at segments 3–5. The legs are black, and the wings are clear except for a small area of amber at the bases. The **females** are dull yellow-brown overall; sides of thorax have thin black lines along the sutures; legs black; wings clear except for a small yellow patch at bases. **Similar species** Very similar to most *Sympetrums*. The black legs separate it from all but *S. danae* and *S. depressiusculum*** (see under those species for differences). The 'waisted' abdomen of the male and the blood-red, rather than orange-red, colour help to separate it on sight from *S. striolatum*. **Habitat** In Britain, this species is almost limited in habitat to well-vegetated ponds, especially with Reedmace *Typha* or Bur-reed *Sparganium*, or ditches on levels. Occurs occasionally in slow rivers and in larger lakes. It seems to prefer water of about neutral pH, and may occasionally tolerate brackish conditions. Elsewhere in the area, outside the UK, it is much more tolerant and occurs in large lakes or small ponds, rivers, canals, and other habitats, with varying acidity. **Behaviour** A typical *Sympetrum*, very similar to the other 'red' species of the genus. They are not as aggressively territorial as other dragonflies, and can occur at high densities in a site. The males are conspicuous and quite easily approached, usually flying only a short distance. They settle frequently on vegetation or on the ground, especially if light-coloured, and even on papers, feet, cameras, etc. Mating begins in the air, as the male seizes the female, and then continues on the ground or on vegetation. Egg-laying takes place in tandem, with the male gripping the female behind the head. The pair jerk rhythmically together as the female scatters the eggs over the water or into mud, usually choosing well-vegetated shallows. **Larval stages**The larvae are usually weed-dwellers, in shallow water. They are active, and development is rapid, taking place in under one year. Length about 18 mm. **Status and distribution** Widespread in England, but this species has declined considerably in the last decade, though there are signs of a very recent revival. A notable species in Britain. Elsewhere in the area, it is widespread and common throughout, and may be the most abundant dragonfly at a site, though its frequency declines in the north of the area.

*Sympetrum depressiusculum**

This species is very similar to *S. sanguineum* in all respects except that the wings are more finely veined (i.e. there are more cells) especially in the lower half, and the abdomen is distinctly compressed dorsoventrally (in contrast to the more cylindrical abdomen of *S. sanguineum*). There are also consistent minor differences in the genitalia. It is not recorded in the UK (though could easily be overlooked), but it is widespread through lowland France, southern Germany, and the Low Countries.

*Sympetrum meridionale**

A mediterranean species which migrates into the area. Its legs are distinctly yellowish or brownish in both sexes and the side of the thorax lacks any dark markings.

▲ *Sympetrum sanguineum* ♂   ▼ *Sympetrum meridionale* ♀

Sympetrum flaveolum   The Yellow-winged Darter

Size Abdomen length: 22–26 mm. Wingspan: 55 mm. Flight period July to early October. Description Very similar in shape and size to most other red Sympetrums, but distinguishable visually by the large amber wing patches covering one third to one half of the wings, especially on the hindwings, at the bases. Males have a brownish thorax and a bright red abdomen without a marked 'waist'. Legs are black with longitudinal yellow stripes. Females are pale yellow-brown, like most female Sympetrum species; wings as males with additional amber patch at the nodus (the break, halfway along the front margin). Similar species Readily distinguished from all other Sympetrums by the wings. Occasional specimens with reduced coloration would need microscopic examination, but these seem to be very infrequent. S. striolatum an perhaps S. sanguineum are most likely to be confused. Habitat In Britain, most likely to be found in small well-vegetated ponds in sheltered places; elsewhere in the area, it breeds in bogs if not too acid, fens and lush meadowland with small ponds such as fishponds. There is an overall preference for tall ungrazed vegetation. Behaviour Typical of other Sympetrum spp. but much more likely to settle on tall vegetation, usually halfway up a stem. It flies weakly, usually for short distances, and hunts mainly over vegetation rather than water. Larval stages Analogous with S. sanguineum and other species. Status and distribution In the UK, a rare vagrant, mainly to southeast England; apparently non-breeding. It is widespread through the rest of the area, tolerably frequent and occasionally abundant.

Sympetrum fonscolombii (S. fonscolombei)   The Red-veined Darter

Size Abdomen length: 24–28 mm. Wingspan: 60–65 mm. Flight period May to November (June to August in the UK). Description A beautiful species, with distinctive red-veined wings, with a bluish tinge. Males are predominantly bright pinkish-scarlet on the abdomen (more like Crocothemis (see page 126) than the other Sympetrums), with abdomen not 'waisted' markedly. Thorax brown-red, segment one of abdomen black, segment two partially black in triangular shape. Wings clear bluish (except for basal yellow patches), but with numerous red veins including the costa. Legs black striped yellow. Females are similar in wings and markings, but thorax and abdomen brownish-yellowish. Similar species A specimen with most wing-veins red is quite distinctive; if fewer veins red, the species could be confused with other black and yellow-legged red Sympetrum species, or with Crocothemis. Habitat In the UK, this migrant is seen most frequently on medium or large lakes with reed fringes. Elsewhere in the area, it breeds in a wide range of still water habitats, including brackish sites. Behaviour Similar to others in the genus, but more likely to be seen hawking out over water in warm weather, when the wings are visibly bluish. It roosts in tall marginal vegetation. It is a strong-flying regular migrant, which can turn up almost anywhere. Larval stages As S. sanguineum and others. Development is very rapid, and there may be two generations each year. Status and distribution A rare migrant, and occasional breeder, in the UK, apparently becoming more frequent (probably because there are more observers). It breeds in France and south Germany within the area, where it is frequent, and migrates northwards from there.

▲ *Sympetrum flaveolum* ♂   ▼ *Sympetrum fonscolombii* ♂

Sympetrum striolatum   The Common Darter

Size Abdomen length: 25–30 mm. Wingspan: 55–60 mm. **Flight period** Early June to October or November. **Description** A rather nondescript species, duller than most other red *Sympetrums*. Legs black and yellow striped in both sexes. The **males** abdomen is red with a few black markings, and marks on the dorsal surface of eight and nine greatly reduced; slight waist at segments 3–5, less than in *S. sanguineum*. Thorax brownish with yellower stripes sometimes visible; lateral sutures with thin black line around them. Wings clear except for small amber patch at base, and scarlet attachment points. Black mark between eyes not extending down sides (see fig. 46a). The **females** are very similar to others of the genus; dull yellow-brown on abdomen and thorax; segments of abdomen often look more distinctly separated than in other species. Facial black mark as in males. **Similar species** In England, most likely to be confused with *S. sanguineum*, though the black legs, more 'waisted' abdomen, and redder colour with more black on segments eight and nine in particular should separate the latter. *S. nigrescens* (see under that species) is a problem in Scotland and Ireland, and intermediate specimens will need referring for expert advice. *S. vulgatum* (very rare in UK) is extremely similar – see under that species. **Habitat** A species of catholic tastes, occurring in almost all forms of still water, including brackish water, bog pools, and neutral or slightly alkaline waters. Also occurs in slow-flowing waters such as canals, and rivers with calm stretches. Not a demanding species. **Behaviour** More aggressive than some *Sympetrums*, the males will attack other males and even larger dragonflies. They settle frequently on vegetation, dead branches or posts, but later in the day, and more generally later in the season, they settle more on warm flat surfaces. The wings are held more forwards in hot conditions. It is a strong flier, most often seen around water, but it also moves into woodland-rides and clearings, or over heathland. The female, as usual, is less obvious and spends more time perched in vegetation. Mating takes place on a perch, and egg-laying is carried out in tandem, as described for *S. sanguineum*. **Larval stages** Very similar in habits and morphology to *S. sanguineum*. **Status and distribution** Very common and frequently abundant in England in a wide range of sites. Rare in Scotland, though overlapping and confused with *S. nigrescens*. Elsewhere in the area, this species is widespread and common throughout, including in mountain areas (up to about 1500 m), as far north as southern Sweden and Norway.

Sympetrum vulgatum   The Vagrant Darter

This species is very close to *S. striolatum* in all respects. It differs morphologically in that the facial black band is prolonged down the sides of the eyes (see fig. 46c and photograph, page 136); abdominal segment one is usually (but not invariably) all black, the sides of the thorax are less obviously yellow-striped, and the vulvar scale of the female stands out at right angles (it slopes towards the abdomen tip in *S. striolatum* see fig. 47). In Britain, this is a very rare (though probably overlooked) vagrant. In Europe it is widespread though they are, rather commoner in the north than the south, and occurring in mountain areas to above 2000 m.

Fig. 47a
Female vulvar
scales,
*Sympetrum
striolatum*

*Sympetrum
striolatum*
♂

*Sympetrum
striolatum*
♀

Fig. 47b
Female vulvar
scales,
*Sympetrum
vulgatum*

*Sympetrum
vulgatum*
♂

Sympetrum form *nigrescens*   The Highland Darter

Size Abdomen length: 24—28 mm. Wingspan: 55 mm. **Flight period** End of June to September or even October. **Description** Very similar to *S. striolatum*, and frequently considered only as a variant or subspecies of it. It differs in the more strongly marked thorax with sutures outlined thickly in black; the increased black markings on the sides of the abdomen and the black forehead mark extending a little way down the eyes (intermediate between *S. striolatum* and *S. vulgatum*, see fig. 46). These all occur in both sexes. **Similar species** *S. striolatum* and *S. vulgatum* are most similar, with the former more likely to occur in similar places. Females and tenerals might be mistaken for *S. danae*, but the black pterostigma, black legs, and black thoracic triangle of *S. danae* are distinctive. **Habitat** Upland or northern bog pools and lakes, often but not necessarily near the coast. Occurs in mildly brackish sites in places. **Behaviour** As *S. striolatum*, though rather less active. **Larval stages** Not studied in detail, but presumed analogous to *S. sanguineum* and *S. striolatum*. **Status and distribution** This species has a very limited known distribution, in Scotland, Ireland and west Norway. Within these areas, especially west Scotland, it is not uncommon but is obviously very demanding climatically.

Sympetrum pedemontanum *

Size Abdomen length: 18—22 mm. Wingspan: 50 mm. **Flight period** July to early October. **Description** A small *Sympetrum*, distinctive for its conspicuously brown-banded wings, with the bands traversing all four wings close to the pterostigma. **Males** have a bright red abdomen with few markings; thorax brownish, legs black, and pterostigmas red. **Females** are the typical dull yellowish-brown, with wings as the males except for yellowish pterostigmas. **Similar species** The banded wings, and weak, low flight make this species readily-recognisable. **Habitat** A species of fens, bogs and wet meadows, i.e. well-vegetated sites with little open water, usually in the mountains. **Behaviour** Similar to other *Sympetrum* species, except that their flight is weaker and more fluttery, and they perch more on vegetation than on the ground (they most resemble *S. flaveolum* in this respect). **Larval stages** As for the genus. **Status and distribution** Very limited in the area, occurring only in the mountains of central Europe, where it is locally frequent at middle altitudes. Unusual amongst dragonflies in being montane but not boreal.

▲ *Sympetrum nigrescens* ♀   ▼ *Sympetrum pedemontanum* ♂

Genus *Leucorrhinia*   The White-faced Dragonflies

A genus of five species in Europe, all of which occur in Northern Europe. They are small, slender, low-flying dragonflies, with small dark brown patches at the bases of the hindwings, short squarish pterostigmas, and white faces. The following key separates the species (close examination is necessary for some). Only *L. dubia* occurs in the UK.

Key to species of the genus *Leucorrhinia*

1   Abdomen strongly 'clubbed' from segments six to nine. Pterostigmas of male white above, dark brown below. A blackish species with blue pulverulence on abdomen segments three to five   *L. caudalis** (page 142)

—   Abdomen not 'clubbed'. Pterostigmas not white above in males   **2**

2   Anal appendages of both sexes white. Labium with white spots on sides. Mainly black species with some blue on abdomen on mature males   *L. albifrons** (page 142)

—   Anal appendages black. Labium entirely black   **3**

3   Distinctive large pale yellow triangular spot on seventh abdominal segment of male; pterostigma black in both sexes. Abdomen broad, extensively red in male   *L. pectoralis** (page 142)

—   No yellow spot on segment seven as described. Pterostigmas red-brown in males, darker in females   **4**

4   Costal nerve yellow-brown except at extreme base; more robust insect, often more red   *L. rubicunda* (page 142)

—   Costal nerve black as far as nodus, yellow brown beyond; more slender insect   *L. dubia* (below)

Leucorrhinia dubia   The White-faced Darter

Size Abdomen length: males 24–27 mm; females 21–24 mm. Wingspan: 50–50 mm. **Flight period** Late May to late July in UK, early May to mid-August elsewhere. **Description** Both sexes have a white face, and dark patches at the wing bases, especially posterior. **Males** have thorax black with broad red stripes; abdomen black and thin, well-marked with red on segments 2–3 and 6–7 particularly. Anal appendages black, pterostigmas red-brown, legs black. **Females** very similar shape and pattern, but yellow in place of red (sometimes reddening in old females); pterostigmas rather darker than those of the male. **Similar species** Very distinctive in the UK, though teneral *Sympetrum danae* are similar (see page 130). In Europe, *L. pectoralis* and *L. rubicunda* are most similar (see Key for distinctions). **Habitat** In Britain, this species has very exacting requirements: shallow peaty pools usually with an active bog margin, and frequently with a heathland surrounding. More widely distributed in north Europe, it occurs in these habitats but also in acid lakes and marshes and is less exacting. **Behaviour** An inconspicuous species, nearly

Paired
*Leucorrhinia
dubia*
(♂ above)

*Leucorrhinia
dubia*
♀

always flying low over the heather or other vegetation, settling frequently. It is territorial, but not aggressively so, and the territories seem to move readily. Males usually hawk over water, frequently returning to settle on the marginal vegetation. Pairing takes place on vegetation, and lasts about half an hour, the pair rising in tandem if disturbed. The female lays alone into shallow water, or onto wet peat or *Sphagnum*. Usually stays close to larval habitat. **Larval stages** Lives amongst vegetation or on bottoms of shallow peaty pools, becoming conspicuous close to emergence time as they gather in the shallows. Length about 20–25 mm. **Status and distribution** A rare and local species in the UK, with a strangely scattered distribution in Surrey, north-west Midland England, and Scotland yet absent from many seemingly suitable areas. It is absent from lowland France, but common in mountain areas (e.g. the Vosges) and increasingly common further north. Frequent in north Germany northwards to south Scandinavia.

Leucorrhinia pectoralis *

Size Abdomen length: 23–27 mm. Wingspan: 55 mm. **Flight period** May to July. **Description** **Males** are distinctive with a broad black abdomen, strongly marked with red except for the *yellow triangle on segment seven*; pterostigmas black, face white, labium black. Anal appendages black. **Females** are more slender, with extensive orange-yellow markings on the abdomen, as far as segment seven (segment seven triangle just visible as paler yellow). Other key features are as the male. **Similar species** Could be confused with other *Leucorrhinia* species, but the males are very distinctive with their broad red abdomen, yellow segment seven triangle and black anal appendages. See Key. **Habitat** A rare species of bogs, peat cuttings and heathland pools or neutral fens in Scandinavia. **Behaviour** Similar to *L. dubia*, perching frequently on vegetation, especially cotton-grass heads. **Larval stages** As *L. dubia*. **Status and distribution** Not in UK. Rare in lowland north France, but slightly more frequent further north through Germany and south Scandinavia. A notable species everywhere in the area, never common.

Leucorrhinia caudalis *

Size Abdomen length: 23–24 mm. Wingspan: 50 mm. **Flight period** Early May to late June. **Description** A distinctive species, with a markedly clubbed blue and black abdomen in both sexes. **Males** Face white, thorax brownish, abdomen blackish, with blue pulverulence on segments 3–5; pterostigma distinctively brown and white. **Females** similar in form with clubbed abdomen, with yellow spots and whitish pulverulence; pterostigmas dark brown. Otherwise similar. **Similar species** Distinctive, by virtue of the abdomen form and colour. **Habitat** Occurs in well-vegetated rather acid waters, including bog pools, heathland ponds, and more acid marshes. Not particularly associated with an active bog moss growth. **Behaviour** Has a very short, early, flight period. Generally similar to *L. dubia*, though more difficult to approach. Males tend to settle on floating vegetation (pondweed, water-lilies, etc) which other species rarely do. Both sexes remain close to the larval habitat. **Larval stages** Active weed-dwellers, taking two years to develop. Length about 20–25 mm. **Status and distribution** Not in UK. Generally rare but widely distributed and locally common in montane areas of north-east France, and south Germany. More frequent further north.

Leucorrhinia rubicunda *

A little-known species, very close to *L. dubia* in habits and morphology. It is slightly more robust, more extensively coloured red on the abdomen, while the thorax has rather more yellow. The costal nerve is yellowish-brown (mostly black in *L. dubia*), and the dark patch on the hindwing may be reduced than that of *L. dubia*. It flies in May and June, in small numbers, in upland areas of north-east France and south Germany; and more frequently from north Germany northwards.

Leucorrhinia albifrons *

A rare and local species, generally similar in colour and ecology to *L. caudalis*, but with a much slenderer unclubbed abdomen, white anal appendages in both sexes, and the labium spotted with white on the sides (all black in the other four *Leucorrhinia* species). It flies from May to June, and occurs infrequently in similar sites to *L. caudalis* from mid-Germany northwards.

ORGANISATIONS RELEVANT TO DRAGONFLIES

In the UK, the British Dragonfly Society, formed in 1983, is *the* organisation concerned with dragonflies, and they offer a link for members to the S.I.O. (Societas Internationalis Odonatologica), the international dragonfly society. Membership details can be obtained from the Secretary, 4 Peakland View, Darley Dale, Matlock, Derbyshire DE4 2GF.

The organiser of the Odonata recording scheme in the UK, at the time of writing, is R. Merritt, 48 Somerby Avenue, Walton, Chesterfield, Derbyshire S42 7LY. Records are always welcome.

All those interested in dragonflies should be interested in their conservation, and this can be best served by joining their local County Naturalists' Trust. Details of the relevant ones are available from RSNC, The Green, Nettleham, Lincolnshire.

Bibliography

Corbet et al (1960) *Dragonflies*. In the New Naturalist series. Collins, London. Reprinted in softback, 1985.

Corbet, P. S. (1962) *A Biology of Dragonflies*. HF+G Witherby. Reprinted by E. W. Classey, 1983

D'Aguilar et al (1985) *Guide des Libellules d'Europe et d'Afrique du Nord, Delachaux and Niestlé*. Paris. (Text in French.)

Dunn, Roderick (1984) *Derbyshire Dragonflies*. DNT, Derby.

Geijskes, D. and Van Tol, J. (1983) *De Libellen van Nederland (Odonata)* Kon. Ned. Nat. Ver. Hoogwood. (Text in Dutch.)

Hammond, C. O. (1983). *The Dragonflies of Great Britain and Ireland*. 2nd ed. revised by R. Merritt. Harley Books, Colchester.

Jurzitza, G. (1978). *Unsere Libellen: Die Libellen Mittel – europas in 120 Farbfotos*. Kosmos, Stuttgart. (Text in German, with colour photographs.)

Nature Conservancy Council (1980) *The Conservation of Dragonflies*. NCC, Peterborough.

Welstead, N. and T. (1984) *The Dragonflies of the New Forest*. Hampshire and Isle of Wight Naturalists' Trust, Romsey.

In Britain, the journals of the British Dragonfly Society have much useful and interesting information. The paper referred to under *Aeshna subarctica* (page 98) is that by Clausen, W. in J. Br. Dragonfly Soc. 1·4,59–67, 1984.

Photographic acknowledgements

Front and back cover, and title page **Bob Gibbons**.

All photographs **Bob Gibbons** with the exception of : Peter Loughran/Hamlyn Publishing Group : 15, 29, 30, 33. Ian Johnson/Natural Image : 117 (bottom). Tom Leach/Natural Image : 59 (top), 62, 83 (bottom), 85 (top and bottom), 89 (bottom), 97 (top), 105 (top), 107 (top), 113 (bottom), 115 (top), 139 (top). **Peter Wilson/Natural Image** : 13, 27, 87 (bottom), 115 (bottom), 137 (top), 91 (top), 101 (bottom), 103 (top), 131 (bottom), 135 (bottom). Simon Davey/Swift Picture Library : 105 (bottom). Geoff Dove/Swift Picture Library : 95 (top and bottom). M. Read/Swift Picture Library : 91 (bottom), 111 (top). M. Hamalainen : 89 (top), 111 (bottom), 139 (bottom). **R. A. Kemp** : 77, 97 (bottom), 101 (top), 133 (bottom).

INDEX of species

Entries marked * do not occur in Britain
Entries marked (*) probably extinct in Britain